I AM STILL HERE!

I AM STILL HERE!

Inspired by The Holy Spirit...

Written By

ADA

Contents

WARNING!!! AS YOU READ AND EVEN TOUCH THIS BOOK/// WARNING!!! GET READY/// WARNING!!!YOUR LIFE WILL NOT BE THE SAME///WARNING!!! YOUR LIFE WILL BE TRANSFORMED AS YOU READ///WARNING!!! READ AT YOUR OWN RISK!!!

"I AM" STILL HERE!

DEDICATION

This book is dedicated primarily to my #1 and only TRUE lover of my soul, mind body and life JESUS, because You: Jesus came to me, my precious Lord and Savior and when You did, You began a lifetime of rescue, restoration and renewal in everything about me. You have transformed my life and continually remind me, what it means to die and live in Christ, (You Jesus) which is gain. You are my friend, role model, teacher, example, my everything, I love you, Jesus Amen.

Father God; You are always with me and You are so faithful and continually keep your promises of never leaving me nor forsaking me and now I am privileged to live for You each day and watch You (Daddy) be glorified in, through, and around me, in the name of your precious Son, Jesus, until His return again. Thank you, I love you, Daddy God, Amen.

Holy Spirit; Spirit of Truth, leading and guiding me daily 24/7, I would be lost without your ever present help. My Comforter, My Guide, My Fire, His Power, His Holiness, keeping me on the straight and narrow path. Thank you. I love you, Holy Spirit, Amen.

To my husband and children, whom have allowed me the pleasures to experience my "Daddy" God through them all; His chosen vessels. I adore you and I am so grateful that Daddy God blessed me by having you in my life and overjoyed to call you family. Thank you for your love, faith and support! May God's love, joy and peace overwhelm you and saturate you daily. I love you, all, Amen.

To my friends and family; brothers and sisters in Christ Jesus. Thank you for your love and patience. Thank you for your encouragement and faithfulness to "Our Father", I know that Daddy will continue to bless you exceedingly and abundantly above all that you can possibly even ask or think. Peace be unto you in Jesus name. Amen.

Introduction: The word of God states that there is a time and a season for everything and this is the time and season now for "Our Father" God to be glorified like never before. God said in the days of Moses and even now that he wants to be glorified in, through and around us. Saints of God we are the vessels of honor, God created and chose to manifest His magnificent and miraculous greatness through. You see, God changes not. God is the same yesterday today and forever more. I am so excited that you will be able to see God and experience Him like never before. I declare and decree that your life, right now, will never be the same as you read this book and are eternally transformed in Jesus name. Amen.

The purpose of this book is to glorify My Daddy (God). To talk about His LOVE, His POWER, His FORGIVENESS, His MERCY, His PATIENCE, His PEACE and everything else about Him. It's not about me and how worthy He made me, yet, How He is with me and will be with you, if you only believe. Believe Him for His Word and TRUST Him and recognize, that HE IS STILL HERE! An ever present help in our time of need.

God is the "Our Father" that you read about, the Jehovah Jireh, Jehovah Shalom, Jehovah Nissi, The Alpha & Omega, The Great "I AM". The God of Terror….Selah! He has so many names, but I call Him (Daddy) in and of my life; wherever I go; in this book. He Is My Daddy and I am His child. So understand when you see Daddy, that is who I am referring to My Daddy, the God of all creation, the God of he universe; My everything, there is none like Him. He is amazing and I can go on and on and on of How Awesome and Great He is, yet, I need to get to the meat of His story. (History)

Remember this book is all about Him in and with me. This is my relationship with Him. Certain, things you need to understand, and I must point out, first and foremost as you read:

- He breathed His own book into existence a long, long time ago and there is no other book like His book: The Holy Bible.
- This book is not a substitute for His Word - The Holy Bible.
- Read His book - The Holy Bible - To Know Him intimately.
- The Holy Bible (His Word) is my source, my truth, my reference.
- This book is written to glorify My Daddy God.
- This book is not religious.
- This book is not politically correct.
- This book will not have a lot of scriptures.
- This book is not about my writing capabilities.
- This book is simple.
- This book is not concerned about grammar.
- This book has parables.
- This book is not full of magic tricks.
- This book is not to convince you to believe.
- The stories, testimonies; experiences you read are ALL TRUE (names may be changed for privacy reasons).
- This book is a LOVE story about Daddy, Jesus, Holy Spirit and me.
- This book and all of its testimonies and many more that are not yet written are all TRUE!

Ultimately, the purpose, motivation and source of this book is LOVE. Daddy God is LOVE. He is my purpose, my motivation and my eternal everlasting source of LOVE. I LOVE LOVE LOVE Him and you know what, He LOVES LOVES LOVES ME AND LOVES you more than you could ever imagine.

God (Daddy) is the same yesterday, today and forever more. Understand that the God of Abraham Isaac and Jacob, the awesome God of Moses, Esther, Elijah and other mighty men and women of God. HE IS STILL HERE! Doing the miraculous, the impossible, the extraordinary, YES and BELIEVEABLE, because of who HE IS and the overwhelming truth that HE IS (STILL HERE) is the GOSPEL (Good News) Like Jesus, this book is full of Good News and I bring you Good News.

Yes the God, who took the form of man (Jesus), to die and to live again and reconcile us back to Himself, for no other reason than the simple truth that HE LOVES US. HE LOVES HIS CREATION. HE LOVES YOU. WHETHER YOU KNOW HIM OR NOT, HE LOVES YOU. HE DOESN'T EVER WANT TO BE SEPARATED FROM US (YOU) EVER AGAIN, BELIEVE IT; IT'S TRUE. Hallelujah!

WARNING!!! AS YOU READ AND EVEN TOUCH THIS BOOK/// WARNING!!! GET READY/// WARNING!!!YOUR LIFE WILL NOT BE THE SAME///WARNING!!! YOUR LIFE WILL BE TRANSFORMED AS YOU READ///WARNING!!! READ AT YOUR OWN RISK!!!

So…sit back and enjoy the journey. Relive and experience Daddy (God's) supernatural miracle working manifestations, not by power, nor by might, but by His Spirit and the blood of Jesus that was shed for you. Receive it into your heart, eyes, ears, mind and body in Jesus name. You too, will experience miracles, signs and wonders, even as you read, Only Believe….WHY? Because that is just the way HE IS! HE IS AMAZING AND HIS WORD, HIS TRUTH, HIS POWER IS UNDENIABLY CONTAGIOUS AND TRANSFORMING. UNDERSTAND THAT BY THE BLOOD SHED STRIPES OF JESUS, YOU ARE HEALED... SO HEALING WILL MANIFEST AS YOU READ; YOU HAVE BEEN MADE FREE; CIRCUMSTANCES ARE CHANGING FOR YOUR GOOD AND GOD'S GLORY. STRUGGLES ARE OVER. NEW GODLY RELATIONSHIPS ARE BEING ESTABLISHED. SUCCESSFUL BUSINESSES ARE LAUNCHING. MARRIAGES ARE BEING RESTORED; FAMILIES ARE BEING UNITED; THE PRODIGALS ARE RETURNING; BY HIS STRIPES, YOU ARE HEALED. CANCER, HIV (AIDS) IS NO MATCH AGAINST THE BLOOD OF JESUS, IT WAS DEALT WITH A LONG TIME AGO, AND JESUS TOOK IT UPON HIMSELF SO THAT YOU DON'T HAVE TO CARRY IT ANYMORE. IT IS GONE, BELIEVE AND RECEIVE YOUR HEALING IN JESUS NAME. ALL MANNERS OF SICKNESS INFIRMITIES AND DISEASE WILL NOT BE ABLE TO STAY IN YOUR BODY ANY

LONGER, AS YOU READ TRUTH, THIS BOOK, IN JESUS NAME. JESUS' BLOOD CLEANSING (STILL FLOWING) AND DADDY'S MIGHTY POWERFUL ACT OF LOVE AND SACRIFICE IS HERE. HE'S ALIVE TODAY, IN YOU, IN ME; THIS IS MY DECLARATION, THIS IS MY DECREE, AND AS I DECREE A THING IT SHALL BE ESTABLISHED IN THE MIGHTY NAME OF JESUS! RECEIVE YOUR HEALING, RECEIVE YOUR MIRACLE, WHATEVER YOUR NEED IS TODAY, THE KINGDOM OF GOD IS AT HAND, REPENT (CHANGE YOUR WAY OF THINKING) AND RECEIVE IN JESUS NAME, AGREE WITH THE KINGDOM OF HEAVEN. IT IS YOUR INHERITANCE. NOW FAITH IS, NOW IS THE TIME TO COME IN AGREEMENT WITH (OUR FATHER) DADDY GOD, HIS SON (JESUS) AND HOLY SPIRIT. HIS WORD, HIS TRUTH AND WHAT HE HAS ALREADY DONE. ALLOW DADDY TO BE GLORIFIED IN HEAVEN ABOVE, IN YOU. HIS BLOOD HAS NEVER AND WILL EVER LOSE ITS POWER. DEPRESSION, ANXIETY GUILT, SHAME AND CONDEMNATION CAN NO LONGER IDENTIFY WITH WHO YOU ARE IN CHRIST JESUS, AND YOU HAVE THE MIND OF CHRIST, BELIEVE AND RECEIVE AMEN. CONFUSION HAS BEEN REPLACED WITH CLARITY. FEAR AND DOUBT HAS BEEN REPLACED WITH HIS PERFECT AND UNCONDITIONAL LOVE, BECAUSE PERFECT LOVE CAST OUT ALL FEAR. HIS PEACE, MERCY, FORGIVENESS AND HIS ETERNAL EVERLASTING LOVE IS YOUR PORTION TODAY, BELIEVE AND RECEIVE IN THE MIGHTY NAME OF JESUS. IT IS TRULY FINISHED.

WARNING!!! AS YOU READ AND EVEN TOUCH THIS BOOK/// WARNING!!! GET READY/// WARNING!!!YOUR LIFE WILL NOT BE THE SAME///WARNING!!! YOUR LIFE WILL BE TRANSFORMED AS YOU READ///WARNING!!! READ AT YOUR OWN RISK!!!

Wherever this book goes; whomever reads this book; as you hold this book in your beautiful hands, or even allow it to touch your body, I declare and decree that Daddy God's anointing and mighty power of the blood of Jesus, by His Holy Spirit will transform your life for your good and His glory in the name above all names, Jesus. He will restore you, and everything about you, after all you were created in His image and the likeness of His Son Jesus. Amen and Amen and Amen.

Now, I know, without a doubt, you are falling in love with HIM already, and if you love Him already, you are excited and falling in love all over again. Taste and see that our Lord is truly good. Daddy be glorified, manifest and let them feel Your Presence! Your Excellence! Your Greatness! Let them see You (Daddy) show them YOUR LOVE, YOUR POWER, HUG ON YOUR CHILDREN, COMFORT THEM HOLY SPIRIT, REVEAL YOURSELF TO THEM LIKE NEVER BEFORE, I love you Daddy, Amen.

If I have provoked you now to know who my Daddy really is, then (Yeah Jesus!) I am on track. I provoke Daddy too and He loves me for it. This book will cause you to ask questions and trust Daddy God; He wants you to ask Him anything and everything. He will answer. Ask Daddy to reveal Himself to you and He will be glad to. To know Him intimately, you must read about (Him) His Word His Truth (Jesus), His Ways (Holy Spirit), His Light. His Life. If and only If you desire a relationship with Him, because he called us to abide in Him, as He abides in us, study His Word. Read about Him. Study to show thyself approved. Don't read His Word (The Holy Bible) just for wisdom and to get knowledge, to get understanding, read it to know Him and understand who HE IS! The I AM! and then you will be able to identify with His Wisdom, His Nature, as it becomes a part of your identity and who you are in Him. His identity in you. Selah!

No matter where you are or the situation you find yourself in. He is there! He is with you! He is just an acknowledgment away! He is a thought away! He is a call away! He is a cry away! He is a prayer (conversation) away! Talk to Him. He is Here and He is standing at your door, waiting on you. Knock! Knock! Acknowledge Him open up and receive. Daddy wants to dance with you, sing with you, laugh with you and yes even cry with you. Daddy wants to love on you. Daddy loves your worship. Daddy loves your praise!

Daddy is not angry with you. I promise you, He is not mad at you! Daddy adores you. Daddy forgave you along time ago. You are forgiven. Daddy wants to fellowship with you and reveal Himself to you. Daddy is a gentlemen. Daddy wants you to take your royal place and inherit His Kingdom on earth, not later, not when Jesus returns. Now! He will not not force you to accept Him. He is waiting on you. You do your part and He will do His. He is faithful! He is a Promise Keeper! You are the apple of His eye and He has your face (picture) in the palm of His hand. Daddy wants to eat dinner with you. Furthermore, Daddy wants to be your dinner (manna from heaven). Taste and see that He is good, yummy for your tummy. HAHAHA...LOLOLOLOL! Daddy loves you and all He wants is for you to open up and love him back!

Although my life is an epistle, (His open book) Daddy God has always been there in my life 24/7. Well of course, Daddy has been with me all my life, duh...He created me. Thank you Jesus. He knew me before He formed me in my mother's womb. It wasn't until later in my life, that I began to acknowledge Him, relate with Him intimately. 35 years now and still in LOVE with Him, Daddy continues to be the air I breathe, my ever present help from the moment He wakes me up to the moment He puts me to bed. Thank you Jesus!

Daddy has done things in many splendid things in my life (openly and behind the scenes). He wants me to share publicly, so that He can be glorified. So join me in glorifying "Our Father" over and over, again and again. Remember this book is not about me it is about My Daddy. A Daddy who never failed me because He is LOVE and (LOVE NEVER FAILS). As you read you will understand and experience Daddy God and see Him for who He truly is., (A PERFECT AND UNCONDITIONAL LOVING AND CARING FATHER). You will love Him in an entirely different way. There are dimensions of God, depths of God, and characteristics of His Persona. He is awaiting for you to learn of Him, so that He can reveal Himself and manifest Himself to you. You will fall in love with Him even more as you continue to read along. I love you Daddy and I thank you. Amen.

I must tell you that this book is special. The truth is that Daddy has been on me to get it finished for some time now. He even said to me, a long long time ago, and I quote "Watch what I am going to do with it", are you watching? I AM. Will I write more?, Well that's up to Daddy (lol). I don't know who is more excited Daddy or me... lol. Truly, it seems like forever to get this book out. Many of my family and friends knew it was coming and were waiting patiently too. Thank you for your continued prayers and support and for your encouragement. I live to edify and encourage you as well. His (God's) TIMING is perfect! Another lesson Daddy taught me, is that sometimes, we think we are waiting on Him, yet, truth be told, He is waiting on us. Selah! Thank you Daddy God for trusting me with your Kingdom and giving me the KEYS! I am overjoyed right now to finally say thank you Daddy, again, for the privilege and the honor to complete it. It is for You, Daddy, I love you and I live in need and dependent on you always. Amen.

Again, I am not religious nor am looking to prove myself to you, nor that I have writing abilities. Get that out of your head. I am having fun. You can have fun in Christ Jesus with Daddy by His Spirit and still be Holy. Daddy is FUN, FUN, FUN and I want you to enjoy yourself, laugh, cry, rejoice, sing, whichever way you are lead to be moved, most importantly, enjoy yourself and be encouraged. I am simply going to share with you miracles; testimonies; incidents; experiences; visions and maybe dreams. If you are learning and reading of Him, for the very first time, I am truly happy for you, trust God it is truly divine and not by chance that you are holding this book in your hand. Daddy has done numerous and many great things in our time together and its time that I give Him a shout out. Go Daddy God! I love you forever. I will shout about Your Goodness and praise Your Holy name in and on the rooftops. So here it is, Amen. All glory and honor to You!

When I was in Redding, CA, visiting an amazing house of worship, during the church service, there was an altar call. Again I am not religious; religion was stripped off me a long time ago. Daddy (in His audible voice) told me and I quote "I HATE RELIGION". Trust Daddy God, when I tell you, any and every ounce of religion was stripped off me, instantly, as He spoke loud and clear. Another mighty woman of God was in the same room and heard Him as well, loud and clear. Believe it! During the altar call which I rarely go to; because I am not a crowd follower, Selah. Daddy said, "Go to the altar". A little hesitant at that time. I've learned, in my relationship with Papa God, now not to make Daddy repeat Himself, over and over again. Can you relate? Again, I've learned, lol. He truly is patient. Hey, Jesus also grew in wisdom, stature and favor with God and men. Amen. So I went to the altar and this mighty vessel, intercessor of God, reached out his hand to grab mine and began to prophesy.

He said, I see this book and it has blank pages. What are you waiting for? Finish it and watch what I am going to do with it. The world is waiting for this book. It will be on the New York Times Bestseller List, saith the Lord, and other beautiful things Daddy shared with me, through this vessel of LOVE. I received the Words from the Lord, hugged Him thanked Him cried a little and returned to my seat. Thank you again, by the way. This book is worth the wait and I pray you enjoy reading it, as I enjoyed writing it. Daddy's timing is everything. Daddy, be glorified in your Son today. I love you and thank you Daddy for your continued patience with me. You are Incredibly Indescribably, Amazing! Amen.

LOVE LOVE LOVE "Our Father", whether you know Him, believe in Him or not, I promise you, you will fall in LOVE with who He is. He is the I AM and He changes not, He is the same yesterday, today and forevermore. Most importantly, He is still here. He loves you and He is even looking and smiling at you right now, as you read, with His heartfelt personified LOVE for you.

Know this! Daddy is OMNIPRESENT. On that note, wherever you are, He is there. In your house, your bed; your living room; your car; your workplace; the bus; the plane; the park; the restaurant; the bathroom; your shower; the hotel; the gym; your school; in prison; etc. Got it? I believed so. Good. Thank you for taking this journey with me and be ready to bless someone else and share this book and allow them to share this journey too. God is still here willing and able to take you to places you have never been to before, not only spiritually, yet, physically, emotionally, financially and beyond. You will have an experience of a lifetime. Remember, God is still here and He is only an ACKNOWLEDGEMENT away.

Brethren, my life is full of miracles, in, through and around me. I live a life now, where daily miracles, signs and wonders is a natural routine occurrence. My life itself is a miracle, sign and a wonder. Although I experience them, every single time, I am in awe of Daddy. It's just something that I appreciate and do not take for granted, nor get used to. I am being transparent. I am overwhelmed and love struck when Daddy God shows Himself faithful. He is Wonderful, so when you are in relationship with Him, it just comes with the territory. You will know soon enough, if you haven't already, and will have firsthand knowledge of what I am talking about. His love is tangible and is shown in many ways. His daily mercy and grace is sufficient for you and me, but when He shows up and shows out, through His Son Jesus, in me and around me, He just truly blows my mind.

Please understand that God is no respecter of person, and what He has done for me He will do for you if you "Only Believe. He is a respecter of Faith. According to your faith (belief) be it done unto you. I have this uncanny childlike faith when it comes to His Word (The Holy Bible) and therefore, I believe like a little child. I am His little child who still continues to believe Him for what He said and what is written in His Word (The Holy Bible). No matter the circumstance; no matter the situation, these testimonies that I am about to share is because I chose to believe. See, I tapped into something great and powerful "JESUS" He is THE WAY, THE TRUTH and THE LIFE, no man comes to THE FATHER but through and by Him. In order to come to Him, you must first believe that HE IS. So I come to Daddy, always believing. I learned that Daddy God is not a respecter of person, yet, He truly is a respecter of FAITH. Amen. Revelation; According to your FAITH be it done unto you. Daddy taught me that not everyone has the same FAITH. There are different levels of FAITH. There is little FAITH, Mustard seed FAITH, Great FAITH, Perfect FAITH, so not everyone has the same FAITH. So when you come to Him (LOVE), believing in

His (WORD) truth, with His PERFECT (Jesus) FAITH (in you) and LOVE (God) NEVER FAILS, all together; miracles cannot help themselves from occurring and manifesting. Selah!

People who have met me and have experienced and been exposed to Daddy's love and tangible anointing power (Grace) upon my life, ask me, how did you get like this??? Truly, truth be told, ITS NOT ABOUT ME, MY RESPONSE: JESUS! They continue to say, I want to be like you. HALT! STOP, NO, NO, NO, NO! WAIT A MINUTE, LETS NOT GET IT TWISTED! Of course, because of LOVE, I take the time to explain and redirect their focus and state the obvious – I HAVE TASTED AND NOT ONLY SEE, YET, KNOW THAT GOD IS GOOD ALWAYS! TO GOD BE ALL THE GLORY, ALL THE HONOR AND ALL THE PRAISE.....

MY RESPONSE: I am quick to let them know. What you see before you is a work in progress, still under construction. See because, My Life coach Jesus is the answer. He is My Example. My Mentor is Jesus!, My Teacher is Jesus! My Shepherd is Jesus. He is my Role Model! My Friend! He is the one I imitate, emulate, copy, pattern my life to. I, die daily to the natural man, so that I can solely live in Christ Jesus and allow Jesus to JUST BE in me. Jesus is #1 to me and He needs to be #1 for you. Seek ye first His Kingdom, His Righteousness and everything else will truly be added unto you. TRUST AND OBEY HIM FOR THERE IS NO OTHER WAY!

Yes, there are many mighty men and women of God in this world, who are anointed and blessed in extraordinary ways, yet, please keep your eyes on Jesus. Trust in no man, only God. I am not the way. Jesus is the way. The way maker lives in me and I know you recognize and feel Daddy's LOVE and see Truth, yet, Jesus is my answer. He is the answer. I refuse to be made an idol or stumbling block in Jesus name. Jesus is the name above every name, including mine. Jesus' Ministries International, Inc. His Ministry, His name and He gave me and you permission to use it. The truth is that I am in LOVE with Daddy, God, Jesus and Holy Spirit, and I do what He tells me to do, I go where He tells me to go, I say what He wants me to say. I am not my own, I am purchased property. You are not your own. We were bought with His blood (Jesus) so keep your eyes on the prize.

MY RESPONSE: Daddy does not want you to be like me, He has me already, He does not want clones or robots. He wants you to give Him Jesus in you, with your uniqueness, the way He created you full of His glory. His DNA is in you not mine; we are from the same mold, yet, totally different. He made you unique and yearns to manifest Himself through your uniqueness. I tell everyone who ask, study the gospels, study the life of Jesus. Matthew, Mark Luke and John. Copy Jesus, be like Him. See Jesus' relationship with the Father, how he spoke and honored and reverenced and ate and slept and cared and loved, etc. His humility, how he healed and set the captives free, how He made Himself of no reputation. How he cried. How he prayed. How He honored His Father (Our Father). How he fasted, walked, talked and so forth. Study Jesus, learn of Him and fall in love with Daddy God and I pray that the greater works will too become a part of your daily life, by Holy Spirit. Amen. Jesus will reveal #1 who He is in you and #2 who you are in Him.

Warning: THE READING OF THIS BOOK WILL TRANSFORM YOUR LIFE AND THOSE AROUND YOU FOR THE BEST, GET READY FOR YOUR NEW JOURNEY AHEAD IN JESUS CHRIST. AMEN.

> Know this: The enemy is defeated by the blood of the lamb and the words of our testimony. If you got a testimony, tell it and continue to keep him (the devil) in his place of defeat. Jesus said, He saw satan fall like lightening (quick and fast). The devil's place is under your feet, fallen and incapable of getting up, in the name of Jesus.

TESTIMONY TIME, AMEN.

IN THE BEGINNING ...

Praise God, as I began to write this book, I was almost completed and the Lord said to me, "Start over and remove the drama". Drama? My response. He said Yes! I don't want my children to think that they have to go through drama or unfortunate events to experience my GLORY, KINGDOM LOVE, MERCY, GOODNESS, KINDNESS, SUPERNATURAL, DIVINE INTERVENTIONS, JESUS, HOLY SPIRIT, JOY, PATIENCE, MIRACLES, SIGNS AND WONDERS, ETC. Selah! Again, this book is about Him, so some stories were left only to glorify My Father in heaven. Maybe I will write about the drama and maybe I won't. Another book, another time, so much to share and thank you Jesus for the time. God's will be done.

CHAPTER 1

Homeless For 3 Days!

I had experienced many traumatic events in my life and like I mentioned before this book is not about me, but to glorify my Daddy God in Heaven. My past does not define me, God, My Father, Jesus, Holy Spirit did and still do. I am not sharing with you so that you can be sad as you read, you won't be able to be sad. The joy of the Lord is truly our strength and if you ever met me, you would not even believe that I had ever been through the fire, because there is NO RESIDUE. Not even the smell of smoke, but of the oil of joy, a sweet smelling scent, and its Jesus' scent. You will see and experience the UNCONDITIONAL LOVE of a perfect Father (Daddy God). He is Faithful and will show up when you least expect it. I share with you of the trials, just to let you know that in adversity, God is still here! He is there! He is everywhere. His strength is made perfect in our weakness. Relationship with Daddy requires dependency on Daddy. If you learn anything from Daddy's Word (The Holy Bible), you will know and learn this one thing: Daddy God cannot and will not go against the WILL of a man. He gave you and I free will. Understand, that he wants us to make sound decisions and even offers us free Wisdom, when we ask Him, yet, He will not go against our will. Even Jesus, had to tell Him, not my will but your will be done and continued the course.

We have options daily, from the very beginning, in the garden with Adam and Eve with the Tree of Life, Tree of Knowledge of Good and Evil. Choose this day, who you will serve....I put before you Life or Death...Blessings or Curses. The choice is yours and Our Father, prefers you choose Life (Jesus) once and for all and follow Him. Although, you have options, it's only the plan of God that will come to pass so submit to His plan. It's truly easy when you trust and obey and allow Him to manifest what has already been finished before it began. Amen.

When making important decisions that will affect you and those around you, seek Godly council. Examine first the PROS and CONS; hear for all warning signs, especially, when they slap you in the face with all kinds of yellow flashes and red flags. You hear an inner voice saying, DON'T GO THERE! DON'T DO IT! BAD DECISION! NOT NOW!, WAIT! YOU'RE NOT READY! LOL. HAVE YOU EVER BEEN THERE? That voice may be Daddy God, Jesus or Holy Spirit. Don't reject Him, Don't reject Truth; and do nothing until you know like you know like you know. LOL. I've been there more than I can ever imagined I'd be. Pray until you have clarity, then trust and obey for the perfect outcome. God will be glorified in Jesus name. Amen.

On that note, a decision I made brought me to the New York City Port Authority Bus Terminal, where I was homeless for 3 days. Yes, little ole me was homeless. With a huge family, yet, no where to go, not because, I couldn't, but because I was truly lost. I found myself at the bus terminal, wondering, talking and asking God, What am I doing here? How did I get here? Why am I here? What would you have me to do? This is not me, I continued to say, I am not a homeless. My family loves me, I have friends that care about me, I don't belong here. I cried out to Daddy God (Hallelujah!) and He answered me, in His loving, gentle, caring and non-judgmental way.

DIALOGUE (The sweet loving voice of My Father): He answered and asked; Do you want My help? I said, weeping, Yes God, of course, I do.

Immediately, God intervened and rescued me. Thank you Jesus, yes, Jesus appeared in the form of an angel and placed me on His eternal path of restoration and discovery and peace and joy and mercy and forgiveness and I received unconditional LOVE and everything else that is good in the Kingdom of God, here on earth, all the time nonstop, even now. Thank you Daddy, I love you, forever, Amen. Thank you for being there, being here, always with me, never leaving me, nor forsaking me. You are my one and only Father God and I am forever grateful. Thank you Jesus, Holy Spirit.

CHAPTER 2

The Angel Of The Lord
(Special Messenger)

This angel was a tan African American gentleman, with fierce yet glorious eyes, who worked at the NYC, Port Authority Bus terminal, He had a uniform too. He worked security. He was kind, His eyes were pure and holy and there was a great peace that came from his spirit that I could not deny. He just came to me and I remember him saying…

DIALOGUE: Young lady, you cannot stay here. I've been watching you and I cannot give you much, yet I have a couch that you can be safe, until you can get the help you need.

Daddy God, said, this is My handiwork, Go! I heard Daddy God clearly and His perfect peace consumed me. I asked no questions, grabbed my bags and obeyed. I tell you, to this very day, I don't know his name and I don't even know where he lives. I was in my body and out at the same time. I was in this world, but not of it experiencing celestial dreams and visions, at the same time. After a week on his couch, safe and protected, I got a job, my own place in Bronx, NY. I went back to the Port Authority Bus Terminal to thank my hero for his kindness. The Security Office said they had no one working there that fit his description. I said, well of course, you do. I was in his house, I slept on his couch, what are you talking about. This was just a week ago. I knew then and I know now, that the God of the universe, the Creator of all things, the God of the impossible was real and tangible and like no one or nothing in this world. I have not yet tried to figure out, what happened, how it happened. I've learned to accept the truth that I will TRUST in the Lord and lean not unto my own understanding. I know without a doubt My Daddy God intervened and I experienced Him in a supernatural way for the very first time. Thank you Daddy God, for being there, here, everywhere, you always are and you will always be. I am eternally grateful. I love you, Amen

Was it the crying out? Was it the very fact I was faced with adversity? Was it that I hit rock bottom? Was I hopeless? No way, Jose! Daddy God had his hand upon my life, all along. He always has and He always will. He never stopped LOVING me. Daddy God was always there, waiting on me to ACKNOWLEDGE Him, so that He can direct my path. I drew nigh to Him as He drew nigh to me. He drew first, when He sent His son Jesus to die for my sins, to reconcile me back to Himself. My Father, My Daddy, My God, My Everything, Oh, how I love you dearly. God had his eye on me all along, you see He never leaves me nor forsakes me. He has his eyes on you too and will not leave you or forsake you. It may appear that you are all alone and no one cares and no one sees where you are or what you are going through, but I am here to tell you, that this is so far from the truth. Daddy cares and He is all knowing and all powerful. He knows everything about you. He knows every hair on your head and even when you lose one, He knows where it falls. He is an ACKNOWLEDGEMENT away. God had plans for me I knew not of, so I know He has plans for you. Seek Him while He made be found of you today. I tell you the truth, Daddy God began the transformation of all transformations, as He continued to guide me and lead me and manifest His blood cleansing power through my life, body, mind and soul. I learned of God, see I knew of God, yet, I didn't really know him. Some of you reading this, may know what it is to know God for real, I am grateful and happy for you. Thank you Jesus. Some of you were taught about a God full of rules and restrictions. A God that is waiting for you to make a mistake so that He can send you to hell. A God that puts sickness on you to teach you a lesson. God forbid. Daddy have mercy on us. I too was ignorant to the truth. I too was taught many wrong things about God and I needed to know Him for myself. Who, He really is and I tell you the truth, Daddy God is good. Know Him personally and reject the lies and rumors about Him. He desires nothing more than for you to inherit and benefit of His kingdom, NOW, not a second later. NOW Faith Is…. He loves you and desires you to LOVE Him back. Again, I needed to know Him for real. I had questions that no one could answer, only God. I was experience supernatural things I did not understand and truly thought I was losing my mind. I wasn't losing my mind, I just traded it for a perfect one (the Mind of Christ) Amen. Thank you Jesus! To know Him is to die to self, my ways, my flesh, my beliefs, my stereotypes and learn His Truth, His Life, His Way, rejecting the lies that were disguised as truths. Can you do that? Will you do that, is the question? Give Daddy, Free will over your life, surrender all to Him and trust Him and see what He will do. Will you dare?

Truly, If you allow Him to take total control of your being, you too will become transparent and people will ask you; How did you get like this? Of course, we know you will respond – JESUS! LOVE! GOODNESS! MERCY! And keep them focused on "Our Father' and His Business (KINGDOM BUSINESS), (ITS ALL ABOUT SOULS) (ITS ALL ABOUT YOU, READING THIS BOOK) (YOUR TRUE IDENTITY IN HIM).

When you are transparent, in all humility, not false humility, true humility; Daddy God, Jesus, Holy Spirit will manifest and everyone around you will know you are different and belong to Him. You don't have to try and prove yourself to them. You don't have to convince them to say the "Sinners" prayer. They will see and experience His Love (Agape) and it just cannot be denied. They will want what you have and will ask, What do I need to do, to inherit eternal life? Yeah Jesus! It's really easy. Just allow Daddy God, Jesus and Holy Spirit to manifest in you and JUST BE! Everyone will be able to see, hear and taste THEM (Trinity) and know that THEY are real and THEY are here and THEY are for you and not against you. I will always thirst and hunger after Him (Righteousness) and He promises to completely satisfy me. Fill my cup and let it overflow continually. Thank you Jesus, Amen. I love you.

God was mindful of me, when I didn't know Him, and God is even more mindful of me now that I do and I am under His employment (LOL), Lordship, Government, Kingdom. I still continue to yearn and search the very height and depth of who He is, because He is great, and wonderful and marvelous, and magnificent and everything to me. He is the very air that I breathe. I cannot breathe without Him nor do I want to. He rescued me from a life of destruction, I would not have a life, if it wasn't for Daddy God, that is why I live for Him. I love Him. He loved me first and you know what I owe Him my life. I am truly grateful, I cannot help not LOVE Him, and it's as simple as that. He is worthy of all my LOVE (His LOVE in me). He is worthy of all the Honor, Glory and Praise. He never gave up on me and He will never give up on you. This book is about Daddy God, Jesus and Holy Spirit and the fact that "I AM" is STILL HERE! He is Here for you. He is here for me. He is here for all. They in us and us in them making our abode one in another. Thank you Jesus.

God is OMNIPRESENT, when He says, He never leaves you nor forsakes you, and He means it. He is always here, always providing, always feeding, always caring, always clothing, always loving, always protecting, always reaching, always calling, always merciful, always forgiving, and always good. He is faithful to keep His Word and bring it to fruition. Trust God and know that He is watching your every move, that He reigns on the just and the unjust, that His Son Jesus died so that you can truly live. He is God; He is worthy and deserves all of who He created you to be. Praise Him for it, believe it and receive it as the gospel truth.

CHAPTER 3

My Encounter With Jesus!

When I was in the New Jersey Air National Guard, stationed at McGuire AFB, New Jersey, I lived on the base and my dorm room was across the hall from Sister K (named shortened for privacy reasons). Oh my precious Sister K, how I love her. She would be (what some people) may label as a stereotypical Pentecostal Christian (long skirts no makeup). Been there, done that, thank you Jesus for REVELATION! Please understand, that I don't judge you for your faith, if you label yourself a Pentecostal Christian, (I love you) so don't judge me (love me). I know one truth and that is (JESUS) and He called us into relationship, not RELIGION. God actually HATES man made religion. He told me. As you continue to read and if I have the pleasure of personally meeting you, you will know that I am very transparent, I cannot help but be transparent, Daddy God made me this way and I am being transformed daily in my mind, body heart and soul. I can express in detail what I mean about being transparent. You would have to wait on the next book for that teaching or download one of "My Daddy's" teachings on-line..Selah. Amen. Understand that I studied "Religions of the World" and I know about the Pentecostal type Christian faith, and a bit familiar with some of the older traditional doctrines and religious rituals, traditions and man made beliefs. All I can tell you right now is, BEWARE! For there is a way that seems right, but the end of it is death. I will share a dream with you at the end of this book.

I was raised by a biological father who was a Born-Again Christian with the Pentecostal doctrine (rooted down in his bones). LOL. I love my earthly Dad and just came back from Mission work with him in Guatemala. I promised him that if he would go with me on mission to Africa, I would go with him on Mission Guatemala, so I did. It was splendid.

Thank you Jesus for REVELATION. As a child, growing up, I was taught of a God full of rules and restrictions and my salvation was based a lot on how I looked, what I ate, when I worshipped, how I talked to God, and felt and I thought God was mad at me, most of the time. Sad, but true, I knew of God, heard of Him (was taught an image of Him and His Nature) but (like I said before) I didn't really KNOW Him. I thought it was pretty hard with all these rules and regulations to even make it into heaven. How could I possibly attain and become worthy, on my own efforts? Appeared impossible. This was so far from the truth. Truth be told, these 6 things I remembered, as a child, growing up about God and stays true to me today:

1. I could call on Him anytime, and He always answers.
2. I am forgiven, so I must forgive.
3. He would never judge me, so I can't judge others.
4. There was nothing impossible for Him.
5. He is everywhere, and He sees all the good and evil.
6. God is Love and He loves me.

OK back to Sister K. She would always come around and invite me to church. She projected happiness and had this unspeakable joy about her, as if she had a secret and it was eternally good (Jesus). She would smile so beautifully, as if to light up a room. She seemed to always be glowing with light when I would see her. If I knew anything about Sister K, she spent time in prayer.

On this life changing evening, I was ill and truly thought I was not going to make it through the night. I had fever, chills and could barely walk. I didn't know what was going on with me. It was not the flu or cold, yet I was deathly sick and needed help. My temperature was 104, last I checked, zombie like and everything I did to relieve this sickness failed. This sickness was not unto death. Hallelujah!

I had checked across the hall earlier to see if Sister K was in her dorm room but she wasn't. I was hoping she would be able to take me to the medical facility on base. I couldn't drive. I was desperate and I remember saying within myself in tears. God, if you are really real, please help me! I am not ready to die. I really need you. I was truly serious about my life, right then and there and the way I was feeling and looking was not good. I CRIED OUT TO GOD! I cried out in desperation. Within minutes, immediately, suddenly there was a knock on my door. Thank you Jesus. A peace came over me as I opened the door to find hope, restoration, forgiveness and most importantly LOVE standing right in front of me in the form of Sister K. Daddy God not only heard me He answered me, immediately, suddenly, quickly. Hallelujah!

I tell you the truth, I jumped on her and grabbed her so tight and pretty much dragged her in my room.

DIALOGUE: I continued to cry and asked, where were you. I didn't want to let her go and I cried out and said to her please pray for me, I need help, please. She smiled and said, Awe! Its ok, Ada don't you worry everything is going to be alright, don't you worry about a thing God got you. You'll be fine come on over here and lay down.

This was what I like to refer to as Divine Intervention. It was no accident that my dorm room would be right across the hall from Sister K, Amen. God all knowing and all powerful, knew this day was coming before I did. Sister K continued to comfort me and layed me down on my bed. She began to pray in tongues, her Holy language smiling and peacefully simultaneously getting a wet hankerchief in the bathroom and wiping the sweat off my brow. I told her I didn't know what happened and tried to explain my condition and she said, just relax spoke peace and said God's got you now. You rest now, while I pray, she continued. I did just that, before I closed my eyes to sleep the last image I had, was of Sister K, kneeled down beside my bed, warring in the spirit and praying for my soul. She was about Our Father's Business and I am forever grateful. Thank you Jesus, Thank you Sister K, for being that mighty weapon in God's hand. Amen.

The dream that changed my life. My encounter with Jesus. My Shepherd. My Redeemer. My Messiah. My Advocate. My Bread of Life. My Healer. As I slept, there He came the King of kings and the Lord of lords in His shepherd clothing. I beheld His glory and I knew who He was and He knew who I was. We were speaking and relating in a way like we had been doing this forever, yet I was meeting Him for the very first time. I was in total peace. Amazingly, He showed me, me in the midst of all the other sheep. There were many sheep, but he showed me how unique and different I was. I stood out; I was set apart, yet, still together, in unity. He said to me, Follow me, I nodded yes, of course, He nudged me a little with his rod towards Himself and I followed. I was concerned because, as I followed I kept tripping and walking with a limp. I kept getting back up as He continued to help. (Ever present help in time of need).

DIALOGUE: I asked Him, why do I keep falling and He continued to guide me and said, behold, look and look again. I looked and the limp was gone and I was walking upright, Hallelujah.

I was overjoyed, yet relieved that He kept helping me and never left my side. Not only did I feel a transformation, the feeling I was experiencing was incredible. Truly indescribable. I didn't just feel perfect. I awoke the next morning totally healed. No fever, no shakes, No nothing. An unspeakable joy was my clothing that morning. Sister K wasn't there either, but I was so excited to thank her and tell her about my glorious dream. My encounter with the King (my love) I was no longer the same. What I felt in His presence was overwhelmingly wonderful and I wanted to experience that for eternity. Questions yes, but I knew Daddy God was still with me and He would answer the questions, in His time. I love you Jesus. Thank you for rescuing me and saving me from me, for Daddy God. I need you more today, than yesterday. Jesus, you are all I need. Thank you, Thank you and Thank you. You are my everything. Amen.

CHAPTER 4

Micaela Means Miracle!

In my military days, I was stationed at McGuire AFB, NJ. My daughter Micaela was about 18 months old. I came home from work and it appeared to be a normal day. I followed the routine of getting off work, picking my daughter up from the babysitter and giving her a bath. When I picked her up from the sitters, everything she ate or drank was in her hair and clothing. She wore it and wore it well. I dropped her off in the morning looking like an angel and picked her up like she wrestled with food and lost the battle. This particular day, I got home and I began to run her bath water, as I usually do. I sat her in the tub and the phone rings. The bathtub was in the upstairs bedroom so I quickly went to answer the phone downstairs.

A dear friend was on the phone and I spoke to her briefly of some issue that presented itself, on this day. It felt as if I was on the phone for a few minutes, but I remember thinking within myself, did I turn the water off? I heard a voice say "My daughter! I told my friend, Olga, I got to go and hung up the phone. I ran upstairs not realizing the length of time I had spent on the phone, it appeared as only a couple of minutes, yet to my surprise, the tub was totally full to the top with water. Mercy! Yes that was my cry, mercy as I fell to my knees. I stared in shock and overwhelming amazement. For those of you, who heard this testimony, you can visualize, what I am sharing. I will try my best to describe it, in detail, for you first time readers. Selah! Truthfully, at that moment, in my condition, I cannot remember to this day (which came first grabbing my daughter or turning the water off). Thank you Jesus.

I could not believe my eyes. My daughter was floating in the middle of the tub, with her head, nose and mouth up out of the water and 1 (one) hand stretched up, straight to heaven as if someone was holding her up. Her body was under water, she wasn't standing, sitting, but floating, at an angle, face up. Believe it! Hallelujah!

I grabbed my daughter out of the tub (still in shock and awe) and began to talk to God. Now, please understand, I have experienced Daddy God in ways that just cannot be denied, but not like this. It became just excitingly natural to talk to Him, as if He was right there in front of me, in human form and I loved it. His attention. His mercy, His peace, His love, His touch, His smile, His voice, His answer and instructions. Yes, as always, I cried out and He answered and spoke to me. His perfect peace continued to keep me focused and calm, flooding my soul with all that He IS. Why did He answer? Because He is a loving Father and I tell you the truth, even when you don't hear Him, or see Him, He is always here. Omnipresent Father, I adore you.

I've had many glorious encounters with God. He is there, even when you don't feel Him. He intervenes, in the most perfect ways and always in the most perfect times. Whether you feel Him or not, He is always working in us, around us and with us. He blesses us with experiences that keep you (us) in total AWE! He is EL-ELYON – GOD MOST HIGH; EL-OLAM, ETERNAL GOD; EL-SHADDAI, GOD ALMIGHTY; JEHOVAH-BARA, CREATOR; JEHOVAH-ELI, MY GOD; JEHOVAH-GO'EL, REDEEMER; JEHOVAH HOSHE-AH, THE LORD WHO SAVES; JEHOVAH-KABODHI, MY GLORY; JEHOVAH MACHSI, MY REGFUGE; JEHOVAH-MAGEN, MY SHIELD; JEHOVAH-MAOZI, MY FORTRESS; JEHOVAH-MEPHALTI, MY DELIVERER; JEHOVAH-ROHI, MY SHEPHERD; JEHOVAH ROPHE, THE LORD WHO HEALS YOU; JEHOVAH-TSIDKENU, OUR RIGHTEOUSNESS; JEHOVAH-UZI, MY STRENGTH; JEHOVAH-JIREH, MY PROVIDER; JEHOVAH-MELECH'OLAM – KING FOREVER…

HE IS supernatural, miraculous, all powerful and most importantly He is real. The Creator of all things…including the water in the tub.

BACK TO THE TUB! Remember, I told you that the tub was totally filled with water, where it began to over flow, yet, my baby, my daughter, my precious gift from Daddy God, Himself. (Micaela) Micki was non-responsive and her face a little discolored. Daddy prevented her from drowning. Yes, God, Jesus Holy Spirit, His angels, an ever present help in our time of need. Daddy God did the supernatural and was waiting for me to do, the natural and finish what He started.

I remember telling God, please God, don't take my daughter (as if He would). **<u>SIDE NOTE</u>: Please stop blaming God for all the evil in the world, He is good all the time, place the blame of evil where it belongs Ex: sin, flesh, satan**. I grabbed her out the tub and held her restless body in my arms, she did not move, yet, I knew she was still alive. I cried out to God and said Lord, what do I do, this is my baby? Her face was a little blueish grey and her eyes were shut. I thought for sure, for a quick second (prison/child neglect) fear continually tried to get a hold on me. I thought for sure that my life was over and at that moment, I was reaping for every wicked thing, in my life, that I had sown. THE DEVIL IS STILL A LIAR! Mercy, said NO! Thank you Jesus! I am forgiven and Daddy doesn't remember the sins. What sins? See, truth is just that, **<u>TRUTH,</u>** in while we were yet sinners, Christ died for us. I didn't understand back then, but I know now, like I know, like I know. Oh taste and see that He (Out Lord) is really truly good.

PRAISE BREAK…HALLELUJAH!

Listen to me please; if you get anything from reading this book, yes, you, I am talking to you! Study and know Him and learn of Him, Amen. Don't study just to prove that you know the scriptures, yet, study so that you can identify with Our Father God and His Son (Jesus) My friend and Savior forever. Your identity depends on it. You in Them and Them in You (One)

God's mercies are fresh and new everyday and I was about to taste it again. Let me tell you what Mercy taste like: God spoke to me and told me, Breathe into her nostrils! Nostrils? Breathe? How about mouth to mouth, like they do in the movies? LOL

Truly, honestly, I needed breathe, myself. I felt faint and still in shock with all kind of thoughts invading my mind. You must trust God, silence the voice of the enemy ad ignore the noise. I said within myself, breathe into her nostrils? I tried to breathe, yet, my breathe was not enough. I tried to breathe again and no response. I was on the ground with my baby in my arms, looking at the mess. I was there, and I wasn't there. I was in my body, but it as if I was watching myself. I was weak. Then suddenly, I felt this overwhelming strength that came from within me and I breathed into my daughters nostrils, with God's breathe, yes, God breathed. It was His because; He is the Breathe of life. He breathed right through me (for my baby) and it was supernatural. A sign and a wonder. Micki, began to cough and a little water came out of her mouth. She was still a little discolored and lethargic, but was breathing. Hallelujah! Thank you Jesus. I was not alone and the journey was not over. I was depending on Daddy God, by Holy Spirit to lead me, comfort me and guide me every step of the way. I am a soldier of the Lord. In His Army. His soldier reporting and following His instructions. God was with me, God never leaves me. God (My Daddy) is still here!

God then had me call Sister M, my prayer partner, to tell her what happened and to get some more divine intervention and assistance. If you don't have a prayer partner, highly recommend you get one and don't leave home without them (lol). Truly, 1(one) can put a thousand to flight, but 2(two) ten thousand. Sister M, I love you. We've known each other forever and still do pray together at any given time. Daddy God, has done many miraculous things with us together so remember her name, you will be reading about her again. Sister Mary, a wise woman of God, heard what happened and told me, " Sister Ada, bring her (Micki) to the church. Understand that, my daughter almost died, by drowning. She was still a little discoloured. Although my daughter was alive, thoughts of brain damage, lung problems, and future trauma, because of this incident had raced through my mind. Those were the facts, yet I followed Truth (Jesus), thank you Jesus.

I asked Daddy God what would you have me to do? He said, Obey. I obeyed. Micki's body was still, a little lifeless. Yet, there was this confidence in the Lord; this calmness; this peace; there was this trust in His Word, there was this Truth (Jesus) ever-present help, in my time of need. I could not deny it. It came and over shadowed me in such a great way. His strength was made perfect in my weakness. Immediately, I threw some clothes on my daughter, packed us a bag and took her to the church. <u>I got to the church and as soon as we were in, praise and worship was going on. Sister Mary was already there. Daddy God said to me, Sit her down and worship me. Praise God, He will never fail me, Jesus is in the house. The joy of the Lord was truly my strength, among other things.</u> I sat her down, began to worship the Lord.

I worshipped God and was lost in his presence. I felt the urge and desire to glance back, at my daughter in the chair, Praise the Lord, Hallelujah! She was renewed, revived and transformed and her eyes were wide open. She was dancing in her seat, with a joy and a happiness, which only God can give. Believe it. Thank you Jesus. The healing provided to us over 2000 years ago manifested on that day. This healing, provided to us from the very beginning. It was truly finished, before it began. Selah! The act of love, mercy, hope was and is still tangible today. God is truly faithful. I share this story with my daughter over and over again and she loves it. My daughter is priceless to me, yet, I am here to tell you that no one loves His children more than we do, but God. Yes my Daddy God loves Micki and your children, more than we do. His love is perfect, unconditional and eternal. I love you and thank you Daddy God, Jesus Holy Spirit for being here and now 24 hours a day 7 days a week, forever.

Micki (Micaela) is now 28 and has experienced a life full of miracles, signs and wonder. She went through school as an A student and graduated high school with honors and several scholarships. She is finishing her Masters Degree in Community Health. All her life,

Daddy God intervened in a supernatural way, especially when she initially began as a tubal pregnancy.

She is healthy and above all, very wise, thank you Jesus. She had no scarring of this incident and it is only because God was and is still here. Your Kingdom Your Will be done in her life in Jesus name. Thank you Daddy God. Thank you Jesus. Thank you Holy Spirit. I love you more and more everyday of your life in me.

I am going to continue to share more and more testimonies to glorify My Father in heaven, only because He is worthy and this is His season. He told me and I quote. "IT IS MY SEASON, JUBILEE! I WILL BE GLORIFIED. I WILL MANIFEST AND SHOW MYSELF FAITHFUL AND ALL OF MY CHILDREN WILL REAP THE BENEFITS OF MY KINGDOM. REJOICE AND AGAIN I SAY REJOICE. IT IS MY SEASON. I AM STILL HERE! WATCH, BELIEVE AND RECEIVE.

Chapter 5

Jesus In The Car!

Praise God, sit back and enjoy, as I continue to share His miracles, signs and wonders. I love sharing this one. You had to have been there. What I am about to share with you, defies science, space and time, but then again, that's Papa God for you. We know that Daddy God, is the Creator of all things and there is nothing that is created that He didn't create. On that note, I will share this miraculous testimony. Let me tell you if I didn't have a witness, I would have checked myself into Bellevue Hospital myself, yet, I had a Brain MRI scan and I promise you, my brain is absolutely perfect. A little humor there. (Lol).

One sunny day after work, My brother and I decided we would go fishing with a friend of his who owned a boat. On this day, my brother went ahead with his friend and took my daughter with him (last minute babysitter) and after work; I was to meet him at the fishing spot. I changed clothes and headed on to the fishing spot to meet my brother. I had an idea of this fishing rendezvous spot, but was not quite sure where it was exactly. I headed out anyway, trusting Daddy God, as always that Jesus is with me. Jesus found me and I will never be lost again. Understand this, most of my life I was never alone, I knew of God and I always felt protected and fearless, so this was and is my mindset. Well, unbeknownst to me, I got lost and could not find the turn that went under the bridge to get to where I was to meet my brother. I began to pray (talk to

God), I was not afraid, yet concerned, because according to my calculations, I should have already arrived at the location and I was not only lost, yet, I did not want my brother to panic, or be concerned for my welfare. Ready for this…listen carefully.

As I prayed to my Daddy God, a car came from the heavens above (Kingdom of God) and appeared directly in front of me. YESSSSSSSSSSS!

Out of nowhere. Listen carefully again, in case you missed it the first time. I was driving and praying to Papa God and instantly, immediately, quickly, and suddenly a car supernaturally appeared before me and I heard, Daddy God say, Follow that car. Hallelujah!!!!!!!!!!! I felt an overwhelming and perfect peace consume me as I heard those words and didn't question, yet obeyed. I was so relaxed, excited, overjoyed and indescribably speechless. This car was dark, blue or even deep purple, wasn't truly focused on the car, yet on the overwhelmingly consuming ILLUMINATING WHITE LIGHT, warm and smiling joyous presence coming out from it.

The make and model I do not know, yet it looked expensive (upscale) and was shiny. As I tried from my car to see inside this car, I saw that there was no human being driving this car. There were no human beings in this car, no angels, absolutely no form of anything, just a GLORIOUS WARM WHITE LIGHT! IT WAS BRIGHT. A light out of this car, reflecting an eminence of warmth, comfort, peace, joy and love. Jesus, His Word, a lamp unto our feet. Jesus the LIGHT of this world, if you follow Him, you will no longer be in darkness.

It was moving slowly to make sure, I kept following. I kept hearing God, say, Keep following, so I did. When it made a left turn, I followed. When it made a right turn, I followed. If I can only explain how I was feeling at the time, words alone are truly unexplainable and glorious. I never experienced a perfect peace like this before and a confidence that God was truly directing my path. Jesus being the WAYMAKER. I continued to try to see what was inside the car, yet, all I saw and felt was the LIGHT. A powerful bright and glowing presence that was all good. This car was projecting a profound power, that was great, strong yet fierce. It was forceful, gentle yet celestial. Again, you had to have been there, words cannot truly express. I remember following it and at the same time I was totally filled with an unspeakable and quenchable joy. The car finally went under an overpass and that's when I realized, Father, God, I am no longer lost, the area looked familiar. I realized that this car was absolutely more than just a car, yet carried the very presence of the Almighty God, My Father, Jesus and Holy Spirit.

The car continued straight ahead and I saw the water, I saw my brother and daughter from a distance. The car continued and when it got to where my brother was, the car turned around and took off, leaving me right in front of my brother as I followed. In amazement, I was speechless, in shock and awe, I could not park the car quick enough to jump out and get my brothers attention. I wanted him to see what I was seeing and experience what I was experiencing as well and to God be all honor, all glory and all praise, he did. Amen.

My brother Elliot, looks towarded my way to see this car coming at him and me behind the car. The car went straight to my brother and when it brought me to my final destination, turned around and left. My brother did not only see the car as well. My brother saw the same and experienced this powerful light radiating from the inside out. As my brother expressed it, and I saw him react, he said every hair on his body was at attention and his mouth was open. He could not believe his eyes and was in a state of shock and said He couldn't move. Understand that this powerful presence was exactly that, powerful. We were captivated. I left my car in park and jumped out the car without turning of the engine and yelled to my brother Elliot, Elliot, did you see? Did you see the car?, He was nodding yes, and tears filled his eyes because He could not speak. He was in utter amazement. The car took off and as it took off, THE LIGHT smiled towards us. Who else would give us an experience like this of a lifetime, but God. Daddy God is truly supernatural and does the impossible. He is still here.

God was truly there. He was in the car. He was in our presence. He wanted to be seen. He wanted to reveal Himself. His power. His comfort. He wanted me to know that He was my guide. He wanted me to see His Spirit. He wanted me to know that I could never be lost with Him. He wanted me to know that He would never leave me nor forsake me. He wanted me to know that He was just a prayer away. An acknowledgement away. Thank you Jesus. I love you Daddy God. You are wonderful, you are great, thank you for being there for me always and forever again and again and again.

After that experience, my brother and I, felt as if we were indestructible. We felt after Daddy God had manifested himself in this way, that there was nothing that we could not do. We were invaded by heaven and loved every second of it so we decided to put on life jackets, and swim across the Delaware River. LOL! Afterall, we felt like superheroes. From our fishing spot, to the distance on the other side of the river appeared very short, so we said hey, we can swim across, why not, if Daddy God is for us, who can be against us? The rip current. (LOL) Truly, we tried to swim, yet the rip current kept bringing us back away from our goal. We needed rest quickly, so Bill came and scooped us out the water into his boat. We will wait until, we can walk on water (like Jesus) and cross the Delaware that way. We will at least be able to enjoy the scenery, in our leisurely stroll. (LOL). What have you ever dreamed of? What would you like to do, if you could right now? Understand, truly know and believe this, nothing is absolutely impossible with and for God. He is worthy of all Honor, Glory and Praise. Thank you Daddy, I love you, Jesus. Holy Spirit continue to have your way with me. Amen.

Warning: THE READING OF THIS BOOK WILL TRANSFORM YOUR LIFE AND THOSE AROUND YOU FOR THE BEST, GET READY FOR YOUR NEW JOURNEY AHEAD IN CHRIST JESUS. AMEN.

CHAPTER 6

Jesus At The Post Office!

Praise God, when I was attending the Book of Acts church in Wrightstown, New Jersey, Sister K, during a prayer session, looked at me and said to me that the Lord told her, I had the gift of healing. As a new born again believer, I was the type that believed everything anyone told me (like a child) as long as they showed me in the Word. If God said it, I believed Him for it. I told Sister K, how do you know this and why is God telling you and not me? I was a bit naïve to the things of God and was just finding out about how God talked to many people whenever, however and how He is God, Sovereign, Almighty, Magnificent and can pretty much do whatever He wants to and how He wants to with who He wants to. Selah! So I finally accepted this and shared it with Sister M and she said,

DIALOGUE: Sister Ada, in her beautiful inspirational tone, if God said it He will confirm it, He always confirms His Word.

A couple days later I was at work, I was in the United States Air Force at the time and I had to mail a box at the post office, where God confirmed His word and did He ever. Praise Him. As I was driving towards the post office and was pulling up to park, I felt like I entered into an entirely different atmosphere. I was there, and I felt myself, parking the car, grabbing the box and getting out of the car (in the spirit realm). I didn't understand what I was feeling, yet, it felt good and my body was a bit tingling. Things appeared a little surreal, yet I knew I was better than OK. As I began to walk toward the post office, the door opened up and this man, he was about 5'8, Caucasian, with blue eyes and his hair was a light brown, kind of thick and up well groomed. He was leaving the post office as I was entering. He stared at me and made a gesture with his hand that his jaw was hurting and he was in pain. I automatically reached out to him and touched his face and said you are healed, go with God. He then looked back at me and smiled. I cannot explain, what happened next, yet for those of you, who believe God for the impossible, and for Him being true to His word and who He is. I tell you this, it happened in seconds, quickly, so suddenly, that I had no time to think, yet could remember about what Sister K, had said to me on the gift of healing and Sister M, saying how God, confirms His word. I proceeded to enter into the Post Office and when I looked back to where the man was standing, where I had this encounter, no one was there. The man disappeared, the man, vanished, the man, that I touched his face and said to him, you are healed go with God, was gone. Vanished. I stood in amazement and awe and I tell you with all that God Is and Was and Is to come, I knew that God just confirmed His word. God confirmed His word with me, through me and wanted me to know of the gift that He had given me. I received it and no one in all the universe can tell me otherwise. Thank you Jesus. I love you Father God forever and ever you are faithful.

Chapter 7

Jesus Heals All!

After, the post office incident, I shared with Sister K and Sister M, the glorious miracle of what God had done. They were so thrilled and excited for me and encouraged me to put my faith to work, so I did. I began to go to hospitals and God healed many, from headaches to cancer, to aids, to asthma, this was over 20 years ago and many times, I thought to myself, would anyone even believe that God is still healing people? I shared with many church folks and believers, what God was doing, God said to me, the world must know, tell them all, so here it is. God says He will be glorified, in through and around us, so God I honor you today and forever more. You alone are worthy and I thank you for my life. He used me and not only as a vessel of honor, yet as His believing and trusting vessel. What a glorious time I was having in the Lord, He healed my nephew's eyes; He healed many that cannot be contained in this book alone. I laid hands on the sick and they recovered in Jesus name. See faith without works is dead and without faith you cannot please God. I was pleasing God and He was being glorified. I believed God and I believed His word and stepped out on faith. Until, I went in to one room and had an experience that took me to another detour in my life, yet that alone is another book, on Spiritual Warfare - you have to get with me later on that. This book is to glorify my daddy God, and to let you know that He was there with me, healing many then and even today. Whatever illness is affecting your life right now, as you read this book; reject the illness and receive, embrace the Truth (Jesus) that by His stripes you are healed and you will be in Jesus name. He is still here. He is with you. Trust, obey and only believe Him for it. Thank you Jesus, I love you Lord. Thank you for being the same, yesterday, today and forever more.

CHAPTER 8

Ovarian Cyst?!

Praise God, Have you ever experienced, God's healing power on yourself, Amen. How many of you can believe God for everyone else and get a word for everyone else, yet find it difficult at times to believe God for yourself, especially when God speaks to us directly, Amen. I know some of you are relating with me here, anyhow...

In my adolescent years, I lived a life without any sickness, and I was very much a healthy person for the most part of my life, after all, God is healing everyone around me and why would I be sick with anything, amen. Well sickness hit very close to home when it attacked my body in the form of an ovarian cyst that was the size of a grapefruit, as diagnosed by the doctors. X-rays showed the cyst and it appeared as a lesion (a large hole in my ovaries). Well I was believing God for my healing, and at times when the pain came upon me so severe, I would pray. I would cry out to God and stand on His word that by Jesus' stripes I was healed. At times the pain would go away and at times, I would call Sister Mary and we would pray through, until the pain was gone. Now the pain I experienced was one that caused me to keel over on the ground, I was at work one time and was rushed to the hospital because the pain was unbearable. It was determined that I needed surgery. No way Jose, surgery was not an option for me, because I've seen, first hand the mighty working supernatural working miracle by and through the work of God, mind you; I AM GOD'S MIRACLE, SIGN AND

WONDER. I had no recollection of ever having surgery in my life. My husband, insisted, so that I not be in pain to persist on me having surgery. I absolutely refused, for sometime, until I gave in, not to my husband, yet, to prove My Daddy God, FAITHFUL. This was my mindset and my rational, that if I can prove to my husband, my Papa God, was (THE PHYSICIAN), I would make a believer out of him (lol). Not that he didn't believe, yet, he didn't want me to continue suffering. Let me tell you again, if you don't know this already, God is not a respecter of person, yet according to your faith, be it done unto you. He is a rewarder and respecter of FAITH. I continue to believe that, if Papa God, can heal everyone around me through FAITH, He can certainly heal me too, with the same FAITH. I told my husband, I am healed and I do not need surgery, this will soon past, watch and see honey.

Well months went by and although the pain would come and go. My condition was getting worst and the pain was more severe. I talked with God and questioned Him on what to do and at times I heard Him, clearly you are healed. Believe me, trust me, You are healed. I would respond, yes Lord, I believe and I know, yet make this pain go away, let my husband know that you are My Healer. I knew within my self, without a shadow of a doubt that I was healed, yet, I would have some severe pains at times and I didn't understand why. Again, I was taken to the hospital via ambulance and that was it. My husband said you are having surgery. Still believing and trusting God for my healing and sharing with Sister Mary, she said well, Sister Ada, I know you trust God, but this may be a testimony for your husband, as well, so I pray you do what God wants you to do. I heard God, through Sister Mary. My God is a good God, He would not heal everyone else and not me, deliverance is the children's bread. Anyhow, I agreed with my husband and scheduled surgery. I told my husband, I will go and you'll see that I am healed. On my way to prepare for surgery and be examined, the doctors took the x-rays and still saw this big old cyst and so they scheduled surgery. On the day of surgery, my husband was with me and we were at the doctors office, I asked him to please stay with me and don't leave my side, I wanted him to be a witness of God's amazing power and see all that was transpiring.

I remember two things on the day of surgery, as explained by the doctor, which was; 1) it was an IN and OUT procedure (same day), and 2) they would go through my belly button and remove the cyst and then release me to go home. As the were preparing me for surgery, I remember looking at my husband with this peace and joy and hope and I said to him, stay with me and watch honey, they are not going to find anything. My husband (smiled) responded saying I am here, I am not going anywhere, I am here with you. When He said this, I heard Daddy God, clear as day, I am here! I will never leave you nor forsake you, thank you for believing Me and He took me into His bosom. I was gone with Papa, as the staff placed the ivy in my vein with anesthesia, to put me to sleep. I was with Papa God, Jesus and Holy Spirit, always together, never alone, in perfect peace that peace that comes from Papa God, Himself, holding on to Jesus (My Healer) and being comforted by My Comforter (Holy Spirit) Thank you, Thank you Thank you, forever grateful. I am eternally yours.

I woke up in the recovery room. My husband was with me and I asked him, where is the doctor and he said, nurse said, he'll be in shortly and he then asked how did I feel and I said I feel great.

Afterward, the doctor walked in with this strange look on his face. Mumbling a bit, confused, in shock and awe, he was shaking his head; checking my x-ray and shaking his head again, looking at me and looking at the x-ray. I knew, like I knew like I knew, he found nothing, so I had to hear him say it, (especially in front of my husband). He began to utter words of apology and I said go ahead doctor, as tears of joy rolled down my face. I knew Papa God, performed a miracle in me, yet the doctor had to confirm it, not for me, but for my husband. His exact words were, after a deep long pause…

DIALOGUE: I am truly sorry Mrs. Hagy, we went in and found nothing, the cyst on the x-ray was gone, we didn't remove anything. If only I did another X-ray before the surgery, all this could have been avoided. There was nothing to take out. He continued to apologize for the surgery and I said no need to doctor, it's OK, My Jesus healed me.

My husband had to hear it for himself, not from my mouth, but the doctor's mouth and I so wanted Daddy God to be glorified. I asked again, so doctor just to clarify, did you remove the cyst? Doctor, replied again, no, there was nothing there, it was gone. I don't know how to explain this, yet, there was nothing there, no cyst, no trace, he began to say I should've taken another x-ray today, before surgery and I am truly sorry that I didn't yet. I said, it's ok doctor, thank you, when can I go home. He said I will discharge you immediately and gave me some after care instructions. Thank you Jesus.

My husband was speechless and said to me, honey, I will never doubt you again, and I said not me, baby, God. God is faithful and he told me I was healed, I believe this was more for you than me honey. Papa God wanted you to believe him too. He is the same yesterday, today and forever more.

Praise God, to date, the only surgery, I ever had. Have had many diagnoses with all kinds of sickness, infirmities and diseases, yet I hold on to my confession, the Word of God, that by His stripes, I am healed. Have I been told by doctors, since then, I needed surgery, most definitely, many times, yet, let God be true and every man a liar. I choose to believe. I believe the report of the Lord and trust Him for my healing everyday of my life. I believe in divine health and although I experience pain and although I feel symptoms that I cannot explain, I believe without a doubt that by the stripes of Jesus, I am already healed. He took every sickness, infirmity and disease upon himself so I don't have to take it. My Daddy God was with me then and He is still with me now. Thank you Jesus, I love you Lord. I love you Holy Spirit, continue to have your way, as we continue to share in His glory, His presence. Thy Kingdom come, Thy will be done on earth as it is in Heaven. There is no sickness in Heaven, allow Heaven to invade your earth.

This testimony didn't end with my husband believing and the doctor as well, this testimony continued to touch the lives of many even until today. The greater blessing came when we went to church, the Sunday after surgery. I was able to share this testimony at church. Surprisingly enough, there was a girl sitting in the audience, during service, who was diagnosed with a cyst in her ovaries, contemplating surgery (lol). You must know that after hearing my testimony and the miracle God performed with me, she was deeply move and touched and decided that she would trust God for her healing and not get surgery. She came to me, in tears, full of joy, full of hope. Christ in us the hope of glory. I thought all along that this miracle was all about me, but it was not; it was bigger than me and affected the lives of many. Papa God is perfect like that. He is good all the time, He is amazingly supernatural and His divine will, will be done, if you allow it. Does my body get attacked? Yes. Have I been diagnosed with many and all types of sicknesses, infirmities and diseases? Yes. Whose report will I believe? His Holy Word, His Truth, what Jesus did on the cross! He is not getting back on the cross. He said, IT IS FINISHED! It finished before it began. The lamb was slain before the foundation of the earth. By His (Jesus) stripes, I am healed. This is my confession and this is my Truth. I will remain healthy in Jesus name and drug free. Trusting and obeying Him (Jesus) the name above every name for there is no other way! Thank you Jesus. Divine Health is my inheritance and it is yours too. Believe and receive it today, by faith...

CHAPTER 9

Daddy God Played With Us!

John 14: 17-21 – God says in His word that God Jesus and the Holy Spirit will make their abode in you and make you a dwelling place, inhabit you. God is faithful who promises and one thing that God will do is confirm His word, He will confirm His truths, He will confirm, who He is and He wants you to experience Him for real. God created you for his pleasure, Amen. Allow; Let; Permit Them (Trinity) to enjoy you as well, by His Spirit. It's easy!

I see myself at times, as God's play toy. If you can remember when you were little and you had your dolls, GI Joes, Barbie dolls whatever game you had and you would just play and play and never get tired. Some of you had dolls that were missing arms or legs and even clothes (I did) lol. You even had games that didn't have all the pieces yet you would still play with them and feel like you can never get enough, you would play and play until, you were satisfied. I believe God is the same way with us, truly. He loves spending time with us and playing with us, just as we are. Remember it was, while we were in sin, that Jesus died for us, not when we had it all perfectly together.

One day, Sister M and I were praying holding hands and praying in the Spirit (Holy Language) Unknown Tongues, etc., and when we opened our eyes, I was standing, where she was standing and she was standing where I was standing, no movement on our part,

31

yet, still holding hands and God played with us. He supernaturally swapped our positions. He played ring around the roses with us and we didn't fall down, just responded in joy and laughter only that He can.

Another day, my natural dad and I (Pastor Angel) were praying and we smelled this sweet, glorious fragrance, which filled the room. My dad, asked, did you just spray something, and I laughed and said no daddy, I am here praying with you the entire time, what you're smelling is Papa God, Himself, His Presence, His Sweet Essence! I was right here beside you on my knees. He said WOW that was pretty strong and smiled and knew without a doubt, it was Papa God. His presence alone smells heavenly. The room was filled with this beautiful unique fragrance, we had never smelled anything like it. It was glorious, powerful, spectacular, amazing, holy, refreshing. It smelled like love filled the air and He refreshed us anew, thank you Jesus. I love you forever and miss your SCENT. Amen.

CHAPTER **10**

Car Accident

Praise God, you know that Christ, while you were a sinner Jesus (He) died for you. I want to share this testimony with you to let you know that, although I was a bit reckless, He was always there for me, I would hear him in ways and at times when I ignorantly did not obey. Remember that "Our loving Father God, always talks to us, yet we don't always listen.

Rev 3:20, Behold I stand at the door and knock… He means that very thing. God is always there, He is a gentleman and will not force himself on you, yet, when you cry out sincerely, He will hear you and He will answer full of mercy. He alone rules and reigns on His mercy seat. He is rich in mercy. Goodness and mercy follow you all the days of your life.

I was driving home one day and flipped over and I totaled my car. Yes, totally destroyed. I misjudged a turn and took it too rapidly. Two other people were in the car with me and as the car was turning over, I prayed.

Not one glass shattered not one broken bone or scratch on neither of us. The car was totaled, the sign was destroyed and I no longer had any tires. All busted at the same time. As the vehicle stopped and I looked around and realized all were perfectly well and there was no loss of life, no bloodshed, no broken glass, I cried… Do you understand? Again, the car flipped several times as it wrapped itself around the sign? All my tires blew and all I had were four rims without tires. This incident happened late at night and no one was hurt. God not only spared my life, but those who were with me. Although traumatic, this was without a doubt a miracle. It could have been worst, a matter of life and death and since God is Alpha Omega and Jesus, the author and finisher of our faith, He said not today, not now, not on my watch. God, Jesus, Holy Spirit was there and is still here today. God loved me and His mercy saved and spared my life along side those of my friends. How amazing is He! He is Love and sits on the throne of Mercy. This same Jesus loves you more than you can ever imagine, I tell you the truth. Thank you Jesus. I love you forever, thank you Jesus for saving me from me.

CHAPTER 11

God Stopped Time

One evening, I was studying for this huge exam, it was an exam that I needed for the military, in order to raise my GT score so that I can qualify to become an officer. My GT score had to be a minimum of 110. I was up studying to the point that I was beyond exhaustion. It was about 2:00 am in the morning. I just began to talk to God, I said I am so tired and You know how important this test and I need sleep but I must finish God. Please help me, I am beyond exhaustion. I need rest. This test is in a couple of hours. I knew I had to take this exam shortly, yet, I also knew I needed rest or I would probably fall asleep during the exam.

Now, listen here, any good student knows that when you are about to take some exams, you need to have a good night, sleep, and eat a well balanced breakfast so that you can be well prepared. Other students find other test preparation methods. As I prayed (talked) to God, I looked at the time again and immediately fell into this deep sleep. I tell you I slept forever and ever and ever and then woke up (bright eye bushy tail) to see, that it was still 2:00am in the morning, same day. Believe it or not. Who would not serve a God like this, who is not contained by space and time? I am here to tell you that I passed that test and raised my GT score and was able to go from a Sergeant and become a Warrant Officer in the United States Army, thank you Jesus. Hallelujah! It was my destiny and nothing can stop your destiny, not even time. God was with me then and He is still here, now. Thank you Jesus, I love you Lord. Amen. God is a supernatural God and defies the very nature, space and time on earth as it is in heaven. He created time. Believe Him for anything and everything. There is nothing that He cannot do, if you ask him believing, you will receive it. Amen.

CHAPTER 12

God Unlocked A Door For A Baptism

One day, we went to baptize a friend of ours, in our home, after church and this was when we went to the Book of Acts church in Wrightstown, New Jersey. I realized I had left my keys looked in the house, yes, we were outside and my keys were inside. We could see them through the window, sitting quietly on the dining table. I was sad and said, my keys are inside and the door is locked…

DIALOGUE: What do we do? Sister Mary said, "O ye of little faith Sister Ada, just tell the door to open. She said it, door open and it did, Praise God.

We went inside and mission accomplished our friend was baptized in the tub and all honor glory and praise to "Our Father God" He made it possible, not by our power, not by our might, but by His Spirit, by faith, by Speaking His Word. The spoken Word. The same way, He created the heavens and the earth, by speaking creation into existence. I stay in AWE of you…Still speechless, when I remember the great and glorious things that He has done. He has done and continues to do great things. He is good and He is faithful.

CHAPTER 13

Two Rainbows

Another time, Sister M and I asked God for a sign and was very specific. We asked for a rainbow and God gave us two, one for each of us, right over our home, it went from the front of the house to the backyard of the house. To this day, we reminisce and share the joys of the many miracles God has done in through and around us. He will do it with you as well if you allow Him to, it gives Him pleasure.

CHAPTER 14

The Finger Of God

We had recently relocated to Florida from New Jersey, my husband, was reassigned to a position in the military. We had to pack up the family and move. We were in Eustis, Florida and I found a position in the Army Reserves. I wanted to be in the military full-time; I had already had about 12 years active duty under my belt and wanted to finish my 20 years of active duty time for early retirement. Waiting on God, I decided to get my Real Estate license (I believe everyone who moves to Florida, has one of these) lol. Truly, I got my real estate license and worked for a real estate company for a year. I then got my Real Estate Broker's license and opened up our own real estate company and did the weekend warrior thing with the army reserves. Now I was content, yet, I wanted to go back to active duty status in the military so that I could retire and then pursue other career options. I applied with several different organizations and continued to do real estate, and trusted God to grant me the desires of my heart.

On this wise, I had a dream that there was a piece of blank paper and it was white and had two (2) names on it. One name I did not recognize, yet the other name was mine for sure I saw my name. After, I saw my name, I said within myself, what is this for? As soon as I asked the question, I saw a great big finger come to the paper and place a circle around my name. This finger was the Finger of God, it was big and white and glowing like fire. I know like I know that it was truly the finger of God and he circled my name. I woke up and told my husband about the dream and he said, Hmm, interesting. My husband learned his lesson with the Ovarian Cyst miracle, and other supernatural things that had happened in my life, he believed more and was eager to find out, what was God up to. Amen. We didn't think much about it and went on with life as usual, yet, for some reason we were expecting. We were expecting something great from God and we knew it would be divine.

One day, I was working real estate when I received a call from US APERSCOM, United States Army Personnel Command and they stated that they had a position for me that was Active Duty, yet it would send me to Chicago, Illinois. I talked to my husband about it and we were knew God brought us to Florida. We did not want to leave. He had his military obligation and I had the real estate, which was going great, and in Christ Jesus, there is always more. I told the administrator on the phone, I would call her back with a decision. We prayed about it and for some reason we felt that God had something for us here in Florida, not Chicago. Again, we believed this is where God wanted us to be in Florida. So me and my husband discussed that we would find out our options and give her our decision. So I called her back and asked her...

DIALOGUE: Maam, What are my options? She said, Well we offer you this position and if you deny it, we put your name at the bottom of the list and you would have to wait until everyone gets a position before we see you again, and hopefully your application will not have expired and so forth and so forth and so forth....You may have to redo your package and so forth, yada yada yada.

I asked her did she have anything in Florida? Why Chicago? I shared with her that my husband is also military and we would like to be in the same state, if at all possible. We have children and family here now in Florida and she said, let me check. She came back and said no, there is nothing else.

I shared my faith with her and told her about my dream with the Finger of God. Furthermore, I told her that I believe God has something special for me here in Florida. She laughed and said to me, you were definitely dreaming. You will have to make a decision now and of course, I turned it down. Sorrowful, because although this job was everything I wanted, it was not in the right state. She heard my sadness and said OK, your name will be at the bottom of the list. I hung up the phone cried, prayed and stayed in God's perfect peace. That peace that comes from Him alone. We felt very strongly that this was the right thing to do. After all, the steps of the righteous are ordered by the Lord and those who are the sons of God are led by the Spirit of God.

Two weeks afterwards, my husband and I were awaken by our phone ringing at 7:00am in the morning. It was a sergeant from the FLARNG, asking for me, Chief Warrant Officer Hagy. My husband answered and I overheard the conversation. It went like this...

DIALOGUE: She is sleep, can I take a message? Who is this again? Ok. I saw his face as he was speaking on the phone in shock and awe and contentment. He said, Yes, Yes. Ok. He then told the sergeant to hold on and said let me talk to my wife. He held the phone to his chest and continued to say. Honey, it is the FLARNG, they have an Active Duty position for you in St. Augustine, Florida, and they said it is yours if you want it. I smiled and said, yes, tell them to publish (cut) the orders.

He responded yes she wants it, she accepts the position. And then He came back to me and asked me, "They want to know when do you want to start? I thought for a moment, because it was during the holidays in 2000 and I wanted to start in 2001, so I said beginning of next year. They agreed and it was done, they told my husband that I would get the orders with sponsor information and phone contacts in the mail. Supernaturally! Divine Intervention. Amazingly! Incredible! Awesome! Majestic!

God brought me back to the dream and told me, I picked you for this job. This is the military. This is the government. This was Headquarters Personnel. I had no interview and they spoke to my husband and not me on the phone. They also asked me when did I want to start my tour of duty. This was in October 2000 and I began in Jan 2001. Afterward, I found out that they had selected another person for the job and for some shocking and unknown reason to them, he turned it down. Hallelujah! God picked me, God picked me. Daddy God showed me His plan, I saw it in a dream and the other man was the other name. We were the last two applicants left to choose from and God picked me. When God (Jesus) says, YES! NOBODY CAN SAY NO! I tell you, God was there for me then and is still here today. He prequalified me; He justified me; He predestined me and He glorified me; for this job. For His will and because He did it for me, He will do it for you, for all. Trust Him and receive your miracle today! Thank you Jesus, I love you Lord.

CHAPTER 15

In People's Dreams

Many times, God has placed me in people's dreams. God has revealed me to people in a dream with purpose. Just like Paul and Ananaias in Acts Chapter 9. I was on mission and it was during this time that Daddy God had drawn me to Himself and had set me apart for a time of transformation, restoration, spring cleaning (or like I would like to believe spiritual surgery). I was in Rhode Island, visiting a friend, in the Body of Christ (Apostle N). I went to a gym, looking for a place where I can do a little exercise, Amen. A woman was standing there at the entrance and kept staring at me. I smiled and said hello and she kept staring at me. As I was leaving she spoke to me and said, I know you and began to ask me had I been there before and than said, she never forgets a face, I know you she insisted. I said well maybe you saw me on TBN. I had been on TBN at least three or four times already. She said, no. I told her well maam, this is my first time here and I am not from this area, I am from Florida. God Bless you, take care and I left the scene.

At my hotel room, God spoke to me and, I heard his audible voice. I truly just love when God speaks to me like that. I begin to look around to try and see where He's speaking from (a little humor there).

He spoke to me and said, she saw you in a dream. I immediately knew he was talking about the lady at the gym. I placed you in her

43

dreams, He continued to speak and said now go and whatever she asks you, release it unto her and I will do it. Yes God. I was beside myself, I know that when I dream, I see certain people in my dreams and in my visions of God and of great things to come, yet, I had never heard of someone knowing me truly knowing me and seeing me in their dreams when they had never met me physically before. It was a bit profound, yet, it was God and that is all I needed to know, to get my instructions from Kingdom Headquarters and carry out my orders, being the good soldier that I am. After all, God's Army is the real one. Amen.

I didn't need to know her dream in detail, I just know what God said, that He had placed me in her dream, for this day, for this season and God was about to fulfill, what He had promised her, using me as His willing vessel of honor. I had all I needed, I had God's marching orders so off I went. I immediately went back to the gym, because it was her place of work and she was not there, I inquired and I was told that she had already left for the day, so I left her my ministry card and wrote in the back of it "Please call me, it's urgent". Praise the Lord the next day she called me and left me a message that she was returning my call and that she would be at the gym. I went and told the JMI Team that was with me, we must go back, I must share with her what God told me and release to her what she needed. We went back and when she saw me, the spirit in her knew, what God was about to do. The Spirit of the Lord was upon me and the power of God was all over me and as she looked at me weeping, I told her, I know now. You saw me in your dreams and she cried out YES. I cried to and spoke and said, ask God anything, God said to ask Him anything and He sent me here to release it to you. She said hold on and went to the back room of her office. She came back with her Bible and some pics that were in her Bible to show me. We were both in amazement said she wanted her husband and her family to serve God. Now I thought for a moment, WOW, God said, ask anything and she asked nothing for herself, yet for the salvation of her family members and I was truly in awe and I said, are you sure that is all you want. Too Easy. She said, wholeheartedly, YES, as she began to show me pictures of her family. Praise God, and I said in the name of Jesus, it is done unto you. Before the end of this month, your entire family, your entire household will be serving the Lord. As I released this declaration, I had a vision of her husband sitting down in the living room intensely ready the Bible and I shared with her. She was overjoyed. I invited her and her family to the conference as well. We hugged, laughed, rejoiced, praised, worshipped and thanked God together.

When she got home from work, that same evening, she found her husband sitting in the living room....YES... Hallelujah! Reading the Bible. She invited her husband to the conference and I was able to meet him. Truly Amazing what the Lord has done. Thank you Jesus. The joy of the Lord was truly their strength. A couple days past, and as I was on my way back to Florida from Rhode Island. She calls me on the phone. She wanted to share with me how she had spoke to her kids and they were so open to hearing about Jesus and she knew without a doubt that the Lord had intervened in a supernatural way. I reminded her of The Word of God in Acts 16:31, when you believe in the Lord Jesus, you and your household will be saved. God is faithful to His promises. His promises are Yes and Amen. We just have to agree and confess His promises for ourselves. Praise God, you are faithful and I thank you for answered prayers and for being there for me, for us, on that day and for still being here for me today. You loved me first and I pray to respond in LOVE daily. Amen.

The second instance was quick, short and sweet, yet it was God and still worth the ink to write and publish it, Amen. I was in Florida, when I walked into a Christian T-Shirt store, off of King Street in Saint Augustine. The owners were Mark and Robin and I had walked in the store because I needed some Christian Polo Shirts for JMI and I was told that there service was good and prices reasonable. I went in the store and when I went in, the Spirit of the Lord was upon me and I began to prophesy to Robin and afterward, she said, I know you and I had a dream with you and I dreamed you came in and did exactly what you just did. Praise God, I almost couldn't believe it, until she went into detail and knew my name Ada, before I shared it with her. She said that God had placed me in her dreams and I would come and I would prophesy and I would keep praying for her. She further said there were things that she believed God had for me and her to do for the Kingdom of God together. This happened over seven years ago and I still go to her with business and I still pray for her and her family. She just made some wonderful Team Jesus T-shirts for us that we wear when we travel on mission and are out ministering. I look forward to what Daddy God has for us to do together always in God's timing, always God's will. Thank you Jesus, I love you Lord. Amen.

In Africa, I was asleep in my hotel room during another miracle crusade and as I slept, I saw this woman in African gear. She was sitting at the table of her hotel room and had some documents in front of her. She was jus sitting there as if she was waiting for someone. I was sleep and had this vision of a woman sitting in her hotel room with her door wide open waiting for me. The Lord woke me up and said go now to her she is waiting for you. She knows who you are and is waiting for you. I woke up and got dress quickly, and began to walk as the Holy Spirit led me. I went down the hall and lo and behold, here is this woman, the Lord showed me in my dream. She was sitting there exactly like I saw her and she saw me began to weep ad asked me to come in. I said here I am, to be honest I had no idea, what I was suppose to do or say until, I got closer and I was waiting on Holy Spirit (Messenger Download). She had some documents on the table in front of her. They were government documents. Important government documents. Contracts, national agreements and as I opened my mouth Daddy God filled it and spoke.

DIALOGUE: Sign them, its OK, you have my permission; It is a good thing and much needed for your country. She said, Yes Lord, and than said thank you to me. I told her all will be well and wished her peace.

Our meeting was short and sweet. All I knew is that she was an Ambassador of some sort and was so grateful and emotionally overwhelmed, as was I, with Our Father's faithfulness, direction and supernatural intervention. Always on time, always mindful of everything about us. Thank you Jesus for being Lord over anything and everything throughout creation.

CHAPTER 16

God Said "I Hate Religion!"

Praise be to God (My Father) Who WAS and IS and IS to come.... So here I am in Africa and I must tell you, if you don't already know, God hates religion! Yes, He told me himself and I will be the first to tell you, being raised Pentecostal and taught about religious traditions, doctrines and customs. Truly, confession is made unto salvation. Deliverance is the children's bread. Father says, if you confess your sins (faults) He is faithful not only to forgive you, but heal your land (to me, that is everything about me, that I have revelation of in areas of my life where I needed to be liberated). To make a long story even longer, I was religious (like the Pharisees and Sadducees), Thank you Jesus for my freedom. Who the Son sets free is free indeed. Father God is so merciful. Thank you Jesus.

Warning: Get Wisdom! Get understanding! Daddy God will not have you ignorant so if you don't know something, pertaining to the Word of God, it is not God's fault. He is not to blame. Truth be told, it is yours based on the Word of God. God has given us all things that pertain to life and godly living. Wisdom is the principal thing, you need it to function in the things of the Kingdom, once you know, knowledge is powerful. Ask God for Wisdom and He will give it to you freely. Ask Him anything according to His will and He will give it to you. He will answer you. He wants you not only to know the Truth (Jesus) but to believe and receive the Truth (Jesus).

I was in Africa with an Apostle friend of mine when she was ready to go and (minister). I was in the back, checking on her needs. Loud and clear as day, I hear (I HATE RELIGION). No, it was not the Apostle and no one else was around, it was God (My Father) Our Father. It was so loud and so absolute that it shook everything around me, about me, mind, body and soul. I looked at the Apostle and she looked at me and I said all teary eyed, because Papa's voice truly shook every part of me. She said Yes. I repeated to heard what I just her God say to me and she laughed and said, Yes, I heard it too. She continued to say, "He hates religion"! I am sure she was laughing at my reaction, not what we heard. I just received straight from the throne of God, straight from My Father's heart and in His audible voice. I HATE RELIGION. That alone was all I needed to hate it as well. That day, I purposed to study religion. I wanted to truly understand and know why He hated it so much. I studied religions of the world, only to find that religion separates man from God (Our Father). Religion divides, when Jesus came to Reconcile; Restore; Remove; Realign, Redeem us back so that we would have a Relationship with Our Father, Jesus and Holy Spirit eternally. It cost Him everything. I definitely had my mind made up that I would do my part to hate religion as well. Know that God didn't create us to be religious robots, yet to be in relationship with Him. He called us to be like Jesus, who came against religion and said what His (Our) Father would have Him to say and do. I began to acknowledge my ways and discern every habit every act every deed to ensure that religion was not a lifestyle for me but relating to the Word of God in my life, through the life of Jesus. It is truly in Him (Jesus) that I live and breathe and have my being (existence). I purposely examined myself, not by my own strength, but by His word and his power and his might, as he continued to give me revelation in this area. Are you religious? Examine yourself and ask Daddy God to transform you. He will I promise you with revelation comes transformation. You will never be the same in Jesus name.

See it was the religious folks that always tried to trap Jesus and have Him prove who He was, when He knew who He was. It was the religious folks that never believed He could do anything. It was the religious folks that challenged Him day in and day out and thought they were better than him and above all that Jesus represented. It was the religious folks who wanted to stone a women caught in adultery, as if they had the right to. It was the religious folks who said Jesus was the son of the devil. The religious folks were blind guides, they could not see Jesus for Who He really Was and Is and Is to Come.

If you are religious, as you read this book, I break that religious spirit off of you in the mighty and powerful name of Jesus Christ. It doesn't matter what religion you claim to be I break in the name of Jesus and break every religious curse that would have gain entry through generations both in your mother and fathers side in the name of Jesus. I declare it broken and cancelled in the name of Jesus. I command every spirit of the Pharisee and Sadducees to leave you now in the name of Jesus. Every legalistic domineering and controlling spirit comes out in Jesus name. Loose your hood on the person reading this right now in Jesus name. I command that Jezebel and Ahab spirit to the feet of Jesus. Have your way Lord. The Lord rebukes you. I release the Spirit of Love, Truth, Power and a Sound mind to fill and saturate every part of your body from the top of your head to the souls of your feet in Jesus name. I loose the fruit of the spirit; Love; Peace; Longsuffering; Faith; Goodness; Gentleness; Meekness; Temperance; as stated in Galatians 5: 22-23. I bless your life and the life of your family in Jesus name with every spiritual and celestial blessing. I declare and decree the mind of Christ to infiltrate your mind and become one. Your Kingdom come Father God, Your Will be done in Jesus name, Amen. Holy Spirit have your way. It is not by power nor by might but by The Spirit of the Living God. Hallelujah! It is finished! Thank you Jesus Amen.

CHAPTER 17

Mute Wife/
Deaf And Crippled Husband

Frenchie and Greg two amazing individuals, who God used to bless me and them simultaneously, Father God is amazing like that. Well how it all went down was, of course supernatural, yet, would you expect less.

It was Lake County, Florida in a small town of Eustis, when I entered into McDonalds to get a quick cup of coffee. I was approached by this young tiny little elderly lady, who was truly elegant in appearance and sweet as can be. Divine encounter once again. This was not by chance but destiny in the making. She saw my Real Estate Nametag "Good Faith Realty, Ada Hagy, Licensed Real Estate Broker, in white red and gold lettering and pointed to it and pointed to me, pointed to it and then pointed to me again, I nodded yes, and smiled can I help you. She put her hand up and signaled for me to wait as she grabbed a photo out of her uniform pocket, this was a picture of her house. Yes she had a picture of her house in her pocket. She smiled and showed me her and again, pointed to the house and pointed to me and pointed to my Real Estate nametag and my wise conclusion caused me to ask, You want me to sell your house? She nodded yes and hugged me like I won a grand prize. LOL. Truly, I did, but did not realize it at this point in time.

Frenchie began to write her address on the back of the picture and gave it to me and I told her I will come by, we understood each other and she hugged me, like she knew me forever. I knew at that point this was God in His miraculous way intervening on behalf of this Frenchie and her family. Of course, out of love, because that is the only way He operates, with no alterior motive, or hidden agendas. He caused our paths to meet and WOW, wait until you continue to read what happens next. Any other Real Estate agent who are in it for the money, themselves and not for the real reason of protecting the public, would have ran, or referred them to another person who can sign language. God was in this totally and had a plan. I had to walk in the Spirit so that His perfect plan can be manifested on earth, in the natural, in this situation and did it ever. God knows best and knowing that God was definitely in this situation. He made it all exciting in every way and knowing that Father God was about to be glorified, had me focused. He knew that I would give Him all the Glory all the honor and all the praise. I could never have pulled off what transpired without Him. He overwhelmed me and I love Him everyday for that. Strange as it had seemed, we understood each other supernaturally only that God can. Frenchie began to sign to me and I just nodded my head ad shrugged my shoulders and than we began to write on a pad of paper in order to communicate with one another. She had a handkerchief around her neck and pulled it down and showed me that she had a hole in it. Truth and facts of this testimony: I will be brief and hit the main points and you will see God's divine and miraculous intervention unfold.

- Went to Frenchie's house to assess and see her house she wanted to sell.
- Met with her husband Greg who was blind and wheelchair bound.
- Reviewed their banking documents, in which they were already in foreclosure status.
- Home had Foreclosure notice to pay or be out with 2 weeks left.

- Their only family was a dog named Shorty and had no other relative around to help them or where they could move and live.
- There home was in disarray.
- I had just had my Real Estate License for about a month.
- I truly was clueless and did not know where to begin.

I spoke with the Top Real Estate agent Shirley where I was working and discussed the situation with her. She told me to contact the Foreclosure representative and explain to him that I had just listed the property to sell and I needed more time. So I did just that and contacted Mr. Frank.

DIALOGUE: Hello Mr. Frank, I am Ada Hagy with ERA, and I just listed the home to sell and I need your cooperation. Abruptly, He responded, they need to pay by the date on the notice or will be put out in the. Sir, please be merciful. They have no where to go. They have no family. She's mute and He is blind and wheelchair bound, Lord God, I need a miracle, please help us. He laughed and said, There is absolutely nothing you can do and "GOD, NO, NOT EVEN GOD CAN HELP YOU!

My Lord My Savior, I said within myself, Daddy God, did you hear what this man just said (lol). Truly, I believed because I know like I know like I know, God was about to show up and show out, Hallelujah! I believe God was just provoked to do Good, only because He is Good, all the time. I went back and shared my conversation and shared what happened with Shirley and she instructed me to call the Mayor, the Press and the TV News. Praise be to God, it did not take all of that, within a week I had a contract more than what we asked for and not only was I able to sell their home, they bought their next home and paid cash. Hallelujah! Thank you Jesus! How do you like them apples! LOL. My God is awesome. Thank you Jesus! Thank you Holy Spirit. Incredible. We adopted their dog only because they could not have pets in their new home, but Shorty was in good hands for sure. There is absolutely nothing IMPOSSIBLE for our God.

CHAPTER **18**

God's Mouthpiece

There has been numerous times, countless times. I truly lost count and cannot think of every single time God had me speak and see things spoken come to pass. God has used me as His mouthpiece, to say, what thus sayeth the Lord. Prophetically, to prophesy of things to come; By decree; to declare and release things to people and watch them come to pass to the honor and glory of God. God told me be careful of what I say, and to choose my words wisely, for as I say it, it will come to pass. As I speak I am declaring law. It may seem a bit over zealous and or too confident for some of you, but I call it (Spiritual Boldness) (Agreeing with the Word of God) It may even appear arrogant and haughty to some of you, but I am here to say, I know whom I am in Christ and I am not ashamed of the Gospel of Jesus Christ, nor His power, nor his might. As God has said, in His Word, death and life are truly in the power of our tongue. Not because of who I am, but Who He Is, in me. My confidence is always in the Lord.

Even this book, not only did God say, this book, will be on the New York Times Bestseller List. I believe God. I declare and decree that it will in Jesus name. I agree with Daddy God. God said to me a couple of weeks ago, Watch what I am going to do with this book! Why? Because He can, Why? Because, this is not about me, but about My Father, My Daddy, My Papa, Amen. All glory and honor and praise to Him, who sits on the throne. He wants to be glorified in through and around you too, if you allow Him. He desires for you to believe Him for the impossible. For He is the God of impossibilities. God is good, He is faithful. Daddy, I praise you for allowing me to fill these pages with your marvelous works, awesome wonder, glory, honor and praise. I love you Daddy God and I know that you know I do. It is You (Jesus) that I live, move and have my being. Thank you for your love, wisdom, power. Thank you for giving me the grace to finish this long awaited book. Thank you enabling me to finish the one thing in my life that is so worth it. This book all for You and About You. Happy Father's day God, Jesus and the Holy Spirit. Everyday is Father's day. Everyday is your birthday. Everyday to me is Resurrection Day. I love you and thank you for being with me now and forever more. I am always grateful to be your child. Thank you for letting me know that You never leave me, nor forsake me. YOU ARE AND WILL ALWAYS STILL BE HERE! Amen.

Taste and see that the Lord is Good (Gracious)! 1 Peter 2:3

CHAPTER 19

Samuel

Praise God, I was working in the Healing and Deliverance Team in Jacksonville, Florida. One night, after casting out demons in Jesus name, service ended and it was time to go home. My daughter came to me, scared to tell me that Samuel was laying on the ground outside in the front of the building. I said to her show me baby and she took me to him.

My husband was with me and there was a crowd of people gathered around my son. He was on the ground, looking pale and blue faced not moving. Apostle K, was praying over him, yet he would not move. She asked me, is this your son. I said yes. There were doctors nearby, and they were going to call 911 and get him to the hospital. I said, no, He will be fine. God was in control and He is faithful. I prayed to God for help and He helped me every step of the way. God began to speak to me and intervened in a mighty way, as He always does.

My son received the Holy Ghost at five years old and he knew about spiritual warfare. He knew about the healing power of God. So I obeyed God and spoke to my son, I knew His spirit would hear me and I said, Samuel get up and come with me. Although he was unconscious, he heard me and with God's help got up from the floor and proceeded to follow me. I grabbed him and told my husband and daughter, don't worry, God is here and He will be fine, let's take him home. They were in agreement and we got him to the car. He would not open his eyes, nor speak. He was also moaning.

God continued to instruct me and said put him in the back seat with you and I did. Pray in the Holy Spirit and I did, all the way home. My husband drove and my daughter, Micaela was in the front seat with my husband. I was in the back seat with my son praying in Tongues. The commute was bout 45 minutes to an hour depending on traffic. This is from Jacksonville, Florida to St. Augustine, Florida, where we lived.

My son would not open his eyes, nor speak, and his head was moving around like he had no control of it. I was in perfect peace, because my mind was stayed on thee (Jesus). I knew that Jesus was making a way out of no way. He is the way maker. God was going to help us get to the root of this, by His Spirit. On our arrival to our home, God said, put your son in your bed and keep praying. My husband knelt beside the bed and kept praying and crying out to God. It concerned him to see our son in this condition. He felt so helpless, yet he did not cease from praying either.

As we layed him in the bed, he began to move like a snake. His body began to slither and I began to cry out even harder to the Lord and war in the spirit. I said to God have mercy, Lord, He is just a boy. This was the mother in me because I knew better. God said to me, you know He is not just a boy and I know what he meant by that because, He reminded me that my son, received the Holy Ghost at 5 years old and was God's mouthpiece too.

I cried out to God even more and pray and my son began to manifest in an unusual way. I began to rebuke and command every demonic spirit that I could think of to come out, in the name of Jesus. Nothing happened! My son began to groan even more and I heard the Lord say, Be Still! I immediately silenced myself and heard very clearly, the name Azazel!

Breakthrough! I said out loud you cannot hide now. I command you Azazel in the name of Jesus, loose my son right now in Jesus name. The Lord rebukes you. My son, screamed a horrific yell and began to weep. What had afflicted him had released him and loosed him immediately and he came to himself. I held him and asked, What happened baby? Who did this to you? He said at the church a woman came to him grabbed his hands and twisted them at his wrist and he felt sick afterward and went outside where he collapsed. He then continued to say Mom, she was a witch, I just know it she was a witch and she did something to me. I told him, its Ok, we will return to the church and you show me who she is. We will deal with her then. I researched the bible and searched for this Azazel and remembered seeing a movie with Denzel Washington, named Fallen, where a spirit called Azazel, transferred itself from one person to another. Azazel appears in the Bible in association with the Hebrew translation scapegoat rite. Leviticus 16:8. Also in Enoch 10:8-9. In some traditions of Judaism, Christianity, and Islam, it is the name of a fallen angel. Azazel is also known as a place. Whatever it was, wherever it came from, it was defeated a long time ago in the mighty name of Jesus. We also have been given power over all the power of the enemy. No weapon formed against us will ever prosper. Thank you Jesus. I believe that just like Jesus ask the demon, What is your name? It's important to discern and know as well, in order to set the captives free in Jesus name.

We were able to go back to the church and share with Apostle K, what happened. The witch was exposed and confirmed by Apostle K. I thank God who was there for me to help me and my son. He was there for me then and is still here for me today, always to God be the Glory, honor and praise. I love you Lord and I am forever grateful for watching over Your children, time and time again. I physically had my children, yet they belong to God. They always did and they always will. They are His children until Jesus returns, Amen. Even today, when I tell Daddy God, I love you and He knows I do, I hear Him say, Obey Me! Do you love Him? Obey Him! Action speaks louder than Words, even more so with "Our Father".

CHAPTER 20

Trinity Broadcast Network (TBN) Interview

When I was on TBN, I was being interviewed by Apostle K, the subject was "Why the Devil Hates Women" I won't answer that question right now, yet, you may want to read about what happened in the garden with Eve and the aftermath, Amen. LOL. Well, anyhow, it was an awesome program and was hosted in Jacksonville, Florida. I have learned so much from Apostle K, in the areas of Spiritual Warfare. God says give honor where honor is due and I honor her on today. Amen. The broadcast went well. I was able to share with the viewers, my testimony about what happened with my son, Samuel, as stated in Chapter 17. The greater blessing to me came after the show.

This was my first time on TBN. During the TBN live broadcast, TBN, would have Prayer Partners on the show receiving Prayer Requests. You can call in and receive prayer and/or submit your Prayer Requests. Well to my surprise, a viewing guest saw me and heard my testimony and left a message with TBN for me to call her after the show. She just wanted to speak to me and only me. Praise God, I thought for a moment, what a blessing that someone would want me to call them back. On my way home from the studio, God told me to call her now and do not keep her waiting. I did as Papa God, directed me to. I called and this woman, said, Ada, thank you Jesus, thank you for calling me back. She said, I saw the show and as you were speaking I saw the healing anointing upon your life and God said for you to "Speak the Word Only" and I will be healed. Wow, what manner of faith is this? For her to hear God, believe God, and act on what she heard God say. Furthermore, to expect healing over the phone, just like that.

Well, Holy Spirit had His way, I spoke and declared healing to her body released healing on her body and she was instantly healed. She even stated that her son was a doctor and did everything He could to help her and nothing worked for years. Well, I told her because of her faith, the Great Physician had already made her whole and I declared her healing to be manifested, right then and there. All I did was come in agreement with the Word of God, with the Truth (Jesus), by His stripes we were healed. By His stripes we are healed. She cried, shouted, and immediately told me of the relief she was experiencing in her body. God healed her and she said, she was waiting for this day. It was her day of healing, deliverance and restoration. Hallelujah! God you are the greatest in all of creation. Thank you Jesus – I love you Lord. Amen.

CHAPTER 21

I Want A Husband!

While we were in Port Harcourt, Nigeria, Africa during a Miracle and Healing Crusade; we were awaiting transportation to take us to the field. On this glorious day of the Lord, we were in the lobby and I was with a Pastor. As we sat, I began to speak to the beautiful young ladies that were working at the front desk of the hotel. If you know me, you know I will talk to anyone at least once, to tell them about Jesus, Amen. No one is a stranger nor off limits when it comes to the Gospel of the Kingdom and how Jesus Christ died for all. So I began to speak to the ladies and invite them out to the crusade. They were like no, thank you and I don't think this is for me right now. I'm very busy and not sure and... excuses, everything was told to me under the sun, except what I was hoping to hear, like a YES! Well you know that our God is a gentleman and He stands at the doors and knocks and He will not break your door down. He will not force His way in. He will not bust the door down, Amen. Knowing that God will not go against the will of a man, I wisely said within myself, neither will I. I kept silent.

Josephine one of the ladies working the front desk, was eyeing Pastor T, as if he was candy. She told me I like him. I said, excuse me. She said I like him, is he single? I love a quiet and big man, she stated. I laughed and said, you mean you like a godly man. He is a man of God. She said Oh, even better, you can't find to many godly man around here. Then the other lady began to chime in and speak as well. Oh yes, it is very hard to find a man. I said if you want a godly man, you need to go where godly man go, don't you think? They looked at me in silence and than said, Yes.

I paused for a moment. You just don't want any man, but a God fearing man. A man that loves God with all his heart, mind body and soul. A man that will be able to love you like Christ loved the church. They were listening attentively and was thinking on what I said as I went and sat down.

Divine Intervention: Here comes God.

Release to her a husband, God said. I'm like OK, God, you have to understand, when God begins to speak to me, I need clarity. I need to make sure I understand that I know like I know, what God is telling me to do and there is no confusion. Amen. For My sheep, hear my voice and a stranger's voice they will not follow. You see someone's life is about to be transformed for God's glory and I want to ensure that I carry out my Father's orders with precision. So me and God have like a short dialogue. Which goes like this:

DIALOGUE: GOD: Release to her a husband. ME: Which one of them? Josephine or the tall one? GOD: The tall one. ME: Yes; Lord.

I arose and I pointed at the tall one with the finger of God. I command her to stand up and I said to her. Do you believe God for a godly husband and she replied, with a loud and for sure Yes I do! There was such a true conviction in her words as she spoke. I said get up and stretch your hands towards the heavens. She did. I spoke, in the name of Jesus, I declare and decree and release to you a godly husband. I command your husband to come forth immediately in Jesus name. To my surprise, she jumped up and responded by clenching her hands together, as she just grabbed something unseen and said, I receive it. Hallelujah! Wise woman. Our ride showed up and off we went to the crusade. We experienced miracles signs and wonders at the crusade. People healed of cancer and all other types of diseases. Lame walked. Demons cast out. Deaf heard. Blind saw. It was all so good to God be the glory!

Praise God, it was the **<u>NEXT DAY</u>**, when we were waiting for our transportation to the crusade grounds. I was gladly interrupted in my reading of the book from T.L. Osbourne on Healing, you will know why I said gladly interrupted, in a second. Josephine came to me with urgency and said, "Woman of God," she got my attention and pointed to the man in a suit at the counter. I saw the man and I recognized him to be one of the armor bearers of the Host of the Crusade that we were attending. I responded, Yes beloved. She said you will not believe what is happening. I smiled and said try me and tell me please (in the Joy of the Lord). Something divine and supernatural was taking place, I felt it. She was pointing at him and stated marriage. I said, What are you saying? She truly was in shock and awe and was catching her breath as she stated that this man, pointing at him simultaneously, came in and proposed to my friend (the tall woman) and asked her out on a date. He said He was looking for a wife and that she was his type of woman. Hallelujah! Now I was the one in shock and awe. I thought within myself, I believe, help my unbelief! I was truly speechless as I watch this man continually put his charm on her right before my very eyes. My God, My Jesus, My Savior, My Lord. WOW! Speechless!

Now you must agree, that although we believe God for the impossible, when He performs it, it truly shocks, amazes us, and overwhelms us to see how faithful He truly is. Knowing that we serve a God, that what He promises, he is able to perform it, blows my mind. I looked at the guy and he smiled at me and he had no clue to what happened the night before. He did not realize that he was heaven sent, that he was an answer to a prayer, a declaration that was just released from God for God. WOW! He left and gave her a card. I ran to the lady and said, What was your response? What did you say? She said, I don't like him, he is not my type. I laughed. I said woman of God, you will love him, go out to lunch with him, and I promise you, you will praise God for your godly man. She with the rest of us to include Pastor T, rejoiced. Although it was incredibly supernatural, we were in awe and so pleased with Daddy God. It was not until later on that day, when we saw him again, that we shared with the gentlemen, what God had did. In all confidence, she will be my wife, he stated. She is beautiful and the kind of wife I need. WOW! It's all I can say WOW! WOW! WOW! Thank you Jesus – I love you Lord, Amen.

Praise God, Sister K, wanted to see me and so I scheduled an appointment to meet with her. Now Sister K, is beautiful inside and out and would attract all walks of life, if you know what I mean. Exhausted with all the men callers, she knew deep down in her heart that God had a man tailor made just for her. When we began to pray. I saw a vision with the man that God had for her. I was led by Holy Spirit to share what I saw and what I heard. I saw her husband, clear as day. They had so much in common, they were so much alike in many ways and that amazingly enough she would know him immediately when she saw him. I began to describe the man I saw and she was in anticipation asking me, how does he look? Tell me Apostle. She was so excited, until I described him. He is a mighty man of God. He is thin, tall **dark and handsome**. She stopped praying with me and said, Oh no, Apostle I like light skin men. I said no Sister K, he is not light, he is very dark skin, yet, beautiful. Let me finish, you will know him on these two (2) details. 1. You both share the same exact birthday and 2. You both are the same age. When I was done praying she was a bit disappointed, yet, I told her to trust in the Lord and lean not unto your own understanding. God knows what we need. God will give you what you need and God (Our Papa) knows best.

A couple months went by and I saw Sister K at a church function in Jacksonville, Florida. I saw her from a distance and she was not alone, she was with the tall, handsome, dark man of God. I smiled because it was the same man God showed me in the vision.

Me and my family left after service and were not able to speak with her, yet she called me to confirm the prophetic vision I shared with her. She told me about her new husband, Praise God. Yes, her husband, the man who was with her. She told me they shared the same birthday and were the same age and that's how they knew and got married quickly. I tell you God is good and faithful. She was so happy and said, Apostle it was just like you said. Remember God said, I was his mouthpiece, God revealed and I was His spokesperson for that day. Would you be His mouthpiece? Would you allow Him to use you to speak of things to come? Would you be His Prophetic Voice, being led by His unfailing LOVE, SPIRIT, WISDOM AND KNOWLEDGE? It's easy! Trust Him and let Him have His way with you in Jesus name. Thank you Holy Spirit. Thank you God. Thank you Jesus. I love you for being there and still being here for me today. Amen.

Chapter 22

Eighteen (18) Million Dollar Deal

During mission, I went and stayed with my niece, who had recently given her life to the Lord and she had blessed me and allowed me to stay with her in my old stomping grounds (The Hood). Although, my real home is Heaven, I was born and raised in New York City (NYC). My niece would occasionally tell her friends at work about God, the Gospel and how God had manifested his miracles signs and wonder in through and around my life. She shared with her co-workers about the mission work and the trips to Africa, Germany, Peru, India and so forth. I would tell her and she would then tell her friends and so on and so forth. Her friends, believed they knew me through her, as she shared the testimonies.

One of her co-workers, knew I was in town and asked my niece, if I would be willing to have lunch with her. Her friend wanted to take me out to lunch and meet with me. I knew that this was a setup and God was about to manifest His magnificent power, in a divine way, once again. I was excited so I agreed to the lunch date.

When we met, she was so kind to ask me, what I liked. Jesus Himself said if a man ask for bread, would you give him a stone? Anyhow, I am not picky, and "IF ITS FREE, ITS FOR ME AND I WILL TAKE TWO PLEASE". LOL. Truly, I know what I like. She took me to this wonderful upscale restaurant and we sat and enjoyed God's presence. She asked me about God and my relationship and I spoke to her as one having authority, just like my Jesus. Why? Because I knew who I was, where I came from and who I was representing, Amen. I came with purpose and I already had instructions from My Father. My confidence is in the Lord! Amen.

She said she had heard a lot of great testimonies that my niece shared with her and just had to meet me. To make a long story short God, reminded me why I was there and told me to eat and address the issue at hand. He did not want any time wasted and wanted me to focus on the purpose of the meeting. He was about to transform this woman's life and make a believer out of her. Understand that, even today, Jesus wants people to believe not for just His Word, but for the very works that His Father "Our Father" does. Amen. So I looked at her and said…

DIALOGUE: Listen my love, this is a divine appointment. I know why I am here, so let's get down to the business at hand. What do you need? Now before you respond, think about what you're about to ask me, because you are asking God Himself and He sent me to release it and give it to you. I am His special messenger and today is your day, I am here for you. You can ask Him anything and it is done.

Her eyebrows raised and a look of attentiveness and curiosity at the same time.

Her response: Anything? You mean I can ask anything. I said, Yes, anything. Her response: Just like that? I affirmed, Yes, just like that.

Totally surprised, yet intrigued, she began to tell me about a real estate transaction that she was working on with this other co-broker and how it was not going very well. She stated that she worked very hard on this project and she did not want to lose the deal based on the other brokerage not cooperating. She told me it was a huge deal that involved an 18 million dollar apartment in NYC. Half of real estate commission on that, do the math, a big deal. Understand that she worked for a very internationally known, profitable and major Real Estate company in NYC. I asked her, quite frankly;

What would you like God to do? She said I want the deal for myself, because the other broker, is not doing their part.

It's done! God had me release the Word of the Lord. He then told me to tell her, Don't forget to tithe and give God what belongs to Him. Amen. She agreed and said, Yes, of course. Any other requests, I asked and she said, Wow, in awe, she asked, I get another request? Yes, I responded. She shared and spoke to me about her son and, I declared to her that her son will be fine and gave her a Word of Knowledge regarding her son and that she need not worry. She received all that was spoken and was in full of joy, hope and peace. We finished our lunch and parted ways. Two weeks went by and my niece shared with me that she closed on the real estate transaction and she received just as the Lord God had spoken. Jehovah Jireh (god who provides came through, as always. Thank you Jesus, Amen. I emailed her directly and she confirmed the promises of God, that are Yes and Amen. He is Faithful, only believe. Thank you Jesus for your faithfulness – I love you Lord. For as long as I have breathe, help me always to say, what Thus sayeth the Lord. I will be (Your) mouthpiece, for I love to speak for You. I love to declare and decree the Word of the Lord. It is my honor, privilege and pleasure, in which I find total joy. You are the One who has found me and made me worthy of such honor. I long to open my mouth and have You fill it always, Father God in Jesus name. To me, Daddy God, being Your Mouthpiece is a delightsome and eternal act of manifested faith. I love when You not only speak to me, but when You speak to Your children through me, Your vessel of Honor. I love you much and I will love you until Jesus returns. Thank you Holy Spirit. Thank You for not giving up on me. Thank You for never leaving me. Thank You for always being here for me. Hallelujah! All honor glory and praise be to You forever. Amen

CHAPTER 23

Divine Protection – The Glass Shield

Praise God, In Africa I was on mission with a mighty woman of God, Apostle K and her husband. God sent us there to ordain Apostles and Prophets throughout the nation of Africa back in 2003. Also present was Apostle J, another internationally known man of God.

Apostle K had just finished her sermon, and she had preached on Behemoth, among other things. She began to minister mass deliverance and had received a word of knowledge that there were 7 witches in the meeting and God was going to allow them to convert from being a child of darkness and come into his marvelous light to become children of light. She was praying Spiritual Warfare prayer and people were being set free in the name of Jesus. 5 witches were holding their stomach and repented, renounced satan, as they came and fell at the altar. It was awesome, God was having His way. Suddenly, this witch (appearing like Bigfoot), ran to that back towards me where I was standing. I was praying in the Holy Ghost and I was watching Apostle K, to ensure nobody was going to jump her (LOL) at least not on my watch, Hallelujah! Thank you Jesus. As this witch came at me, as if to lunge and inflict bodily harm. Physically, she was about 6'2 and I am 5'5, but Spiritually, the GIANT was in me, Hallelujah! Truly, she could've probably taken me out, physically, yet, I did know some TAE KWON DO and I would have used it if I had to (self defense and all). LOL. Truly as a soldier I am trained to kill, yet choose to LOVE! GOD IS LOVE!

I cannot help but laugh at times, when I share this testimony, only because she was like a beast. All my life, I had never encountered such a creature. I needed help and I needed it NOW. Now faith came at a greater level, when she came at me growling and her eyes were looking crazy. I thought for a moment that foam was going to spew out of her mouth. She looked wicked. I thought within myself, as she charged at me, My God! I looked to the heavens and quickly called on Jesus. The name above every name. I stood still, I did not move, I was unmovable and steadfast in Christ Jesus.

The moment she got really close to me, I felt a glass shield come from the Kingdom of Heaven, right in front of me. It made a loud thumping noise as it was rooted in the ground before me. The witch hit the glass. Hallelujah, Amen, Thank you Jesus. Yes the witch hit the invisible yet protective hard glass shield that came right in between us. It stopped her right in her tracks, right in front of me. Her face was smashed up against it, right before me. She was paralyzed frozen couldn't move. Picture this: Have you ever seen someone put their face on a glass or breathe on a glass, too funny, but so true, so real. This was her position. She could not move, she felt the glass and could not cross it. I was totally protected, My Daddy God, My Shield, My Strong Tower, My Refuge, My Everything, protected me all the way around. Glory Hallelujah!

Now this glass shield was strong enough to keep her from harming me, yet soft enough to allow me to reach out and touch her full of compassion. Jesus! Come on now, listen, glass shield, straight from Heaven; I was fearless. I was there, but I wasn't there. At that moment, Heaven invaded earth. I was in this world, but not of it. A spiritual boldness saturated me and came upon me at this point.

In Jesus name, as I stretched my hand towards her through the glass shield and touched her full of compassion, she fell to the ground slithered like a snake and was totally set free. She got up and asked what happened, as if she was in a trance. I said Jesus! Jesus happened, give God the glory you are good now. Thank you Jesus. I helped her up and she went along her way, totally set free delivered form the powers of darkness and now a child of His marvelous light. Praise God, almighty, who was, and is, and is to come, Amen, Amen and Amen.

As we were leaving the sanctuary, a woman (the last witch) remember, there was 7, as the Lord revealed to Apostle K. five repented immediately at the altar. 1 was set free as they encounter Jesus in me and than there was 1 left. She came running behind Apostle K, and yelling at her to stop and minister to her at once. She demanded service and she angrily wanted it now. I was walking behind Apostle K, so I stretched forth my hand and stopped her from connecting with Apostle K. Apostle K was done. We were done, the meeting was over. It was clear to us all, that we were to leave. I signaled to her No, not today, we will be back tomorrow. She went away speedily. I thank God for his divine protection, I thank God for Jesus, for His blood that was shed and for giving us power over all the power of the enemy. Know this to be true always, weapons may form, but they will **NEVER** prosper. Jesus is our ever present help in the time of need. I love you Lord, you was there for me in Africa, my very first international mission. You have been with me always. You are still here, today. Thank you, Thank you, Thank you. Be glorified in, through and around me. I submit and surrender to Your Greatness Father God, Jesus, Holy Spirit have Your Way. Amen.

CHAPTER 24

Pastor's Healing And Deliverance

Several years ago, there was a couple here in Saint Augustine, Florida. They were leaders in the faith and currently have a church. I ministered in their church and shared the love of "Our Father" Daddy God. One day the Lady Pastor called me and mentioned that she believes something is wrong with her husband and that he needed deliverance. Please understand that these are pastors and leaders in a church in Saint Augustine, Florida.

DIALOGUE: I asked her, what do you mean, please explain. Well she said at night, when he sleeps, in bed, he growls like an animal I said, you mean he snores and he said no, he growls like an animal. She then said, I believe he needs deliverance from demonic spirits. So I said lets meet at your church and I will bring a team with me, if its ok, with your husband, you tell us when and where.

Meeting was set, my husband and I, our son and two other ministers prayed and fasted and went to our appointment. Ready for anything and everything, we arrived at the meeting and we went into their office. Holy Spirit have your way. Her husband was so happy to see us and greeted us with smiles as usual. Understand, we fellowshipped with him, in the past, and he always appeared and presented himself perfectly normal. Sanctified, saved and fill of the Holy Ghost. He had a smile that would light up a room. He even appeared celestial.

We sat down and had a conversation, in their office at the church. I brought with me a Healing and Deliverance questionnaire I had used to minister to the multitudes. I have seen many totally set free with this questionnaire. I will send you a copy of it and you'll understand why.

I asked the Pastor, if he knew why we were there and he replied, Yes. I asked, Do you mind if I take some notes during our time together, you know, like in a doctor's office. He replied, Sure no problem. So, I asked questions and he responded. Holy Spirit began to have His way. The interview portion was just him and I and his wife. He was very quiet and then I told him, we are done, let us pray. I then called the others in and asked them to pray in the Spirit (Holy Spirit) of course. I directed the pastor to get on his knees for prayer. He looked at me as he began to get on his knees as if he didn't want to get on his knees, yet had no choice. I commanded him to kneel down and bow before the King of Kings and Lord of Lords, he did. I immediately placed my hand on his head and began to pray.

At this time, I began to command the spirits, identified and revealed to me during the interview process, to come out in the name of Jesus. Thousands of voices yelled out of him all at once. His wife (the pastor) ran out the room because the sound was a bit uncanny. We continued to pray. There were many voices within him, speaking at the same time. I commanded them to be quiet for they had no right to speak to me. They responded and said, you ain't got no power. I responded, not by power, nor by might, but by the Spirit of the Living God, you are all coming out in Jesus name. His body twisted in a way that was visually unexplainable. God said to me, do not remove your hand from the top of his head, so I obeyed and continued to command the demons to come out, there were many and LOVE, would not quit, fail, nor give up.

I said to him, during this process, repeat after me, Jesus is Lord and he replied with, "I am Lord". Not. We continued to pray, until my husband, opened up the Holy Bible and began to read John 3:16 and 1 Corinthians 13, LOVE chapter. He wrapped his arms around the pastor and it was over. His hard twisted body crumbled and he collapsed and wept. He was totally set free. Praise be to God! I then said, repeat after me, Jesus is Lord and He responded, with Jesus is Lord and kept thanking Jesus new found freedom. He continued to weep and was thankful. He was grateful. We helped him up to his seat, for he was weak and his voice was soar. We commanded the ministering angels to minister to him and asked Holy Spirit to fill him life, truth, love, peace, joy, every good thing. I watched and spiritually saw angels ascending and descending above him, as rays of light. Speechless.

His face was glowing bright and he had a smile on his face. His countenance had changed right before us. A perfect peace that surpassed all understanding was present in the entire room. Thank you Jesus. Daddy God was there, Jesus conquered death and the grave and Holy Spirit had His way.

His wife came back in the room and asked is my husband Ok. I said to her, Oh yes, he is better than OK. You have a new husband. After that experience, she said, please, I am next, you need to do me and my entire church…lol. I told her she was, fine and taught them the truth about satan, a defeated foe. Most importantly, all you need to know is Jesus said, He saw satan fall like lightening. He fell! Jesus dealt with him so it is now easy for us to keep him in his place of defeat. So cast him out, in Jesus name, anytime he tries to deceive you or anyone else with his ridiculous dramatical manifestations. Satan is a counterfeit. A smoke screen. I share this testimony so that you know…

1. Father God who lives in us created him.
2. We have been given power of over all of the power of the enemy.
3. Satan is a defeated foe.
4. No need to make a ministry of casting out demons alone.

One thing, I did want to add, was that the pastor had no knowledge of what happened. His throat was truly sore and he kept saying that he felt the Fire of God, upon his head, which immobilized him. Thank you Papa God, for loving him and setting him free. LOVE never fails. LOVE made him free. You are an awesome God. Thank you Jesus, Holy Spirit for being here always and forever. Amen.

CHAPTER 25

Some Of You...

SOME OF YOU READING THIS BOOK WILL LIVE AND OPERATE IN THE SUPERNATURAL ON A DAY TO DAY BASIS. THE KINGDOM OF HEAVEN WILL INVADE YOUR EARTH AND EVERYONE AROUND YOU. YOU WILL WALK ON WATER. THE GREATER WORKS, YOU WILL DO BECAUSE I STAY BEFORE MY FATHER, IN JESUS NAME. YOU WILL RAISE THE DEAD. YOU WILL BE A FINANCIAL ESTABLISHMENT TO THE BANKS OF THE NATIONS AND THE WORLD. YOU WILL BE USED TO REACH ENDLESS SOULS FOR THE KINGDOM. THE SPIRIT REALM WILL BE MORE REAL TO YOU THAN YOUR NATURAL ENVIRONMENT. FATHER HAS HEARD YOUR CRY AND HAS ANSWERED. YOU WILL BE SOUGHT FOR THE WISDOM OF GOD THAT YOU WILL MANIFEST. YES, THE KINGDOM OF GOD WITHIN YOU WILL MANIFEST LIKE NEVER BEFORE. RAISING THE DEAD WILL BE NORMAL FOR YOU! YOU WILL CLEAR OUT HOSPITALS. CANCER WILL BE NO MORE IN YOUR PRESENCE. ALL FOR SOULS, ALL FOR LOVE, ALL FOR HIS HONOR, GLORY AND PRAISE. ALL BECAUSE HE LOVES YOU AND HE CAN. YOU WILL CARRY AND LIVE IN HIS GLORY. RECEIVE IT AND BELIEVE IT! IT IS DONE. THE LORD IS YOUR CONFIDENCE. THE AUTHOR AND THE FINISHER OF YOUR FAITH. HALLELUJAH! NEW LIFE!

Father God, thank you for allowing me to release this Word to your people. I did not expect this; yet, I am so privileged and honored. Thank you Jesus. Thank you Holy Spirit. Thank you for Your Holy Presence. Speechless! Amen. Freely I receive, freely I give.

Praise God, I was in Florida and I had just stopped by this church and heard this man preaching in the service. I didn't attend the service, I was just passing through and stopped long enough to hear him say these words. **SOME OF YOU** are going to leave this place and miracles are going to begin to happen around you. Effortless miracles. Because of God's presence alone, in your life, supernatural favor, without trying, miracles everywhere. I heard not just **SOME OF YOU**, I heard clearly, those who have an ear to hear, YOU, and me. I received a Holy Spirit impartation, as those words spoken grabbed me and pierced my very mind body and soul. It was not only an invitation to believe but to taste and see. Taste and experience, His magnificence, His Glory, His Truth, His Ways, His Power, His Glory, etc. Those words penetrated my very being. I heard Daddy God through this man and I received it all for me, by faith.

Immediately after, God called me to Himself, for a time of consecration. I just wanted desperately to be alone with Him and He had plans for me. I shared this experience with my husband and he blessed me to go and obey the voice of the Lord. God wanted time with me to show me, teach me, reveal to me by His Holy Spirit. New Season, New life experiences. New Dimensions. Transformation. Restoration. Revelation. Reconstruction. Reformation. My destiny unwinding and His glory manifesting. Thank you Jesus for loving me the way you do. Thank you Jesus for being the perfect example of love. You know how I feel about you Jesus, what else can I possibly say.

As I traveled, with God, He would speak and I would hear and obey. With God, love and obedience go hand in hand. Please don't ever tell Him you love Him and flat out disobey Him, doesn't work. He is Truth and there is no deceiving Him. He told me what He did not only trust me, but I needed to trust Him. New territory for me. Have you ever lived a life totally submitted to His will? It is possible when you trust and love Him for real. No hidden agendas. No ulterior motives. True love for God, Jesus and Holy Spirit and receive His love not only for you but for others. All mankind. ALL HUMANITY. ALL CREATION. You love Him, because He first loved you. When you know you are loved by Daddy God, it is easy to love with His love. Holy Spirit helps us.

WARNING!!! AS YOU READ AND EVEN TOUCH THIS BOOK/// WARNING!!! GET READY/// WARNING!!!YOUR LIFE WILL NOT BE THE SAME///WARNING!!! YOUR LIFE WILL BE TRANSFORMED AS YOU READ///WARNING!!! READ AT YOUR OWN RISK!!!

CHAPTER 26

KFC

Our journey begins. I stopped in New Jersey to get an oil change. My husband told me to make sure I get and oil change so I stopped in Trenton, NJ, to get it done. The mechanic said it would be about 45 minutes to an hour, so I decided to get something to eat. I love Italian food and I saw a restaurant that I began to proceed in that direction, but Daddy God said go to KFC. Sadly, I obeyed, I truly prefer Italian food over KFC anyday.

Arriving at KFC, I beheld a women just getting her order and going to sit down. I kept watching her for some reason. The same experience I had with the incident at the Post Office was happening again. I was there in my body, but I was not alone. I felt the power and presence of God in an awesome way. I entered the spiritual realm and something great was about to happen. I just knew it. I continued to the counter to order my food. I did not know what to order so in communion with Papa God, I asked within myself, What would You have me to order, now that you have me here. I looked at menu and ordered a chicken bowl, looked harmless enough. I truly was not hungry for KFC, yet I knew I was not there for me. It wasn't about me. God's will. God's plan.

I paid received my food and them lead by Holy Spirit, sat down by the young lady. I sat down about 7 feet away from her to eat and await further instructions. God said, Be still. I watched this women be totally delivered of demons. I did not utter a word to her. I did not touch her, nor did she even notice I was there. She began to weep uncontrollably and the other people in the restaurant just watched as well and did nothing. They looked to me because I was the closest to her and Daddy God said, Be Still. The lady continued to foam at the mouth, growl and then weep. When it was all over which was in minutes. Daddy God told me now get up and leave.

Imagine that. I wanted to console the women and explain to her what I just witnessed. I wanted her to know all is well. Daddy God said, Now leave. I left. He then said, it's not by power nor by might but by My Spirit. My Presence within you. You will carry My Presence and it is more than enough. You don't have to touch struggle anymore with demons, when you show up, I show up. Acknowledge, recognize My Holy Presence and you will experience My Glory like never before. I was like, Yes Sir, Daddy God, deal. How else would one respond? LOL.

Truly, I was so amazed. I never ever in my walk with Daddy God, experience His Magnificent power in such a way. It was personable. It was relationable. It was fun. It was easy. He brought me back to the Word, He spoke through the mighty Man of God, in Florida. **SOME OF YOU**...will with leave this place and miracles, supernatural, signs and wonders will begin to happen, effortless around you. Just because of Who I carry. Who I represent and Who lives in me. The Word of God says, God, Jesus, Holy Spirit abide in us and I abide in them. We are one. I recognized and began to study the Kingdom of God and the Kingdom of Heaven, only to unlock and experience how deep and wide and awesome His love really is. He loves us so much that He would send His Son (Jesus) to die on the cross so that Daddy God would never be separated from us ever again. Jesus reconciled us back to the "Our Father". We are His dwelling place. When you really think about it, how can you not love Him. WOW! Speechless!

CHAPTER 27

Staples

I left there got my car and then proceeded my travels with Daddy God. (About My Daddy's Business) in another dimension. I experienced more of His greatness; trusting in Jesus, dependent on Holy Spirit and hearing His voice like never before.

The journey of discovery and transformation continued...

I stopped at a Staples store and 2 more supernatural incidents happened there.

1. A lady lost her credit card. She came to me and asked, as I was using the copy machine. Excuse me did you see a credit card here? I believe I left it in the machine. I said no maam and Daddy God told me (behold) look. He directed my attention to this man. He showed me the man who had the card. I pointed to him and told her, he has your card go and get it from him. She looked at me strangely and said Ok. As I watched her ask the man, he pulled out his wallet from his pant pocket and gave her the credit card. The women stared at me in amazement.

2. Same lady came back to me and said thank you. Do you mind praying for me? I was diagnosed with a tumor in my head, she continued to say, this is why I am so forgetful. I

immediately grabbed her head and placed my head with hers and said, in the name of Jesus, you are healed. She just smiled and didn't say anything and left Staples, keeping her eyes on me as she was leaving the building. She was looking at me with such a gaze and full of faith. I knew like I knew like I knew that the tumor was no more. We both knew and experienced a divine and supernatural encounter. The Kingdom of Heaven invaded earth again. Don't stop Father God, overwhelm me anytime and anywhere, all day long. Thank you Jesus, love you Lord. Have your way Holy Spirit.

CHAPTER 28

India – Deaf For 10 Years

I went on a mission trip to India. Immediately after sharing the Gospel of the Kingdom of Heaven (Good News), we had an altar call. Several healings took place. A man came for prayer. There is a youtube video floating around, as proof, for those who need help believing.

This man was deaf for about 10 years. He had experienced trauma and could not hear. This was my first mission to India and I was expecting our mighty God to do the impossible. At an altar call, you can see those who have all the faith in the world for their miracle as they come forth. They are determined and they know that they will not leave the same way they came in. Their mind is made up. They have a single eye. Selah! I love to see that in people, it stirs up the faith within me. The truth that they really believe God. They believe the Word. They believe Jesus. Their faith has already made them whole, its' just a matter of timing now. Amen.

My interpreter was translating as I began to declare healing in His ears. I snapped my fingers 3 times and at the 3rd snap, his ears opened. Totally restored. He received his hearing and it happened so quickly. Hallelujah! My interpreter couldn't believe it and kept asking him, is it true? Really? Is it true? Are you healed? Can you hear me? The man repeated what he heard. Jesus is Lord. I told the interpreter, that I was going to deliver him from a spirit of unbelief…lol. Father God is amazing.

Believe me, the words that I speak are true, or if not believe me for the works My Father does. If you are deaf and reading this book. I declare and decree that your ears be open right now in Jesus name. I command every spirit not of the Holy Spirit to loose its hold on your ears, your mind and every part of your body. I remove the lie and release the truth of what Jesus did on the cross over your life. I declare and decree in Jesus name and agree with the Word of God that you have the mind of Christ. Receive it, believe it and enjoy your healing. Thank you Father God that there is no distance in the Spirit. You are there with the reader right now. It's not by power, nor by might but by the Spirit of the Living God in Jesus name. Amen. The deaf hear, the lame walk, the blind see, the dead live again in Jesus name.

CHAPTER 29

Eyes

Father God did miracles within my own family. My nephew was young and his vision was very bad. He did not like wearing glasses. So I asked my sister if I can pray for him. Emotionally she answered yes. She too had faith and you can discern by the response, she expected a miracle. I prayed for my nephew. His sight was instantly restored and my sister expressed tears of joy. On this day his sight is still good and he can see clearly now. No glasses needed. Thank you Jesus! Furthermore, when my brother Elliot was baptized in the name of the Father, Jesus and Holy Spirit, he came up from the water and his brown eyes had temporarily changed to a green and blue eye. For what purpose, you may ask? God knows. We both stared at the mirror and wept. Unexplainable! God is SUPERNATURAL! Only that He can. I don't ask God Why? I've learned to accept and stay in AWE of His GREATNESS! One thing I do know if He desires that I know the why? He will tell me. Jesus is Lord of my family too and has intervened so many times and in so many ways. Thank you Father God, you are so worthy of all the honor, glory and praise. Where would we be without You. I cannot even imagine. Thank you for your love. Help me to show you that I love you always. That my I LOVE YOU are not just mere words. Amen.

CHAPTER 30

Tyler Perry Movie

Praise God, as a child I always had a passion to be in the movies. I wanted to be a famous actress. What child in life did not want to be in Hollywood? LOL Truly, except that desire never went away. For those who know me and have been around me you know MY LIFE IS A STAGE and I stand before an audience of three (3) Father God, Jesus, Holy Spirit.

I had a scholarship to attend Lehman College in New York after high school, yet, I went the other way. I joined the military. After retirement from the military, among many other things, I pursued one of my dreams, in the Entertainment Industry. It had been prophesied that the Lord was going to use me to change the face of Hollywood. I've learned that when Father speaks it happens When Father says this will happen, you can cash the check, it's done. He confirmed and spoke it to me again when I was driving in NYC with my niece. The Lord spoke to me and said, you are going to be in a Tyler Perry movie.

You will be working with Tyler Perry, he is my son too. I had a dream where me and Tyler Perry were with a group of other people sitting at a table discussing a project. Not clear it was TV or Movie or even a play. Yet we were definitely working together and it was good. I pray for Tyler Perry and certain people Daddy told me specifically to pray for. I don't' normally say a lot of the conversations me and Daddy God have, especially when it involves someone else, only because. Daddy God always confirms His Word to the other person as well. Daddy God likes to include us and tell His prophets what He is doing before revealing it. I know that when the time comes, Tyler Perry will know what he has to do. Back to the car, when I heard the Voice of the Lord, I looked at my niece and said, Daddy God just told me I am going to be in a Tyler Perry movie. As I spoke those words they came alive in and out of me. She got "Holy Ghost" chills all over her body. Father God, she said, I believe you. When you said that, I not only believe you, but I too, felt it in my Spirit. We rejoiced in the Lord and went about our day.

Now I know Father God has His children already working in the Entertainment Industry. I met one mighty man of God, just this past year. I know his Spirit and I love him dearly. He represents Father well with his simple true and real self. He is considered as an Apostle to the Stars: Apostle Tim Storey Life Coach. If you are reading this (Tim: brother from another mother, same Father) I honor you. Thank you for your work in the Kingdom of Heaven for souls.

Why would Daddy God pick me? Good question. Total honor and privilege. Whatsoever you want, I surrender over and over daily, 24/7 to your will Father, Your Way, Your Wisdom, Your Mind, Your Holiness, Your Grace, Your Kingdom, Your Truth, Your Love. Thank you Jesus. Hallelujah!

Years later, after military retirement, my daughter and I were upstairs working in the office. She was working on her resume. She too is an actress, model and had several agents. She said, Mom, Tyler Perry is looking for some (background extras) in Georgia.

Living in Florida, not too far away, I said, Hmm, interesting. I didn't have a resume or any photos to submit, yet, I remembered what Father said. My Spirit man got a bit excited. The Lord works in peculiar ways and He will use anyone anytime even my daughter. I told everyone who cared to listen. I am going to be in a Tyler Perry movie. You must understand, I have all his movies. Daddy God told me to pray for Tyler. I have a lot of his movies and attended some of his plays. He's amazing. I love who my Daddy loves and I hate what my Daddy hates (sin). He is on my prayer list. So I said within myself:

1.   I will get a Headshot photo.
2.   Make a resume with my high school, college acting and theatre experience.
3.   Send it and trust Daddy God for the rest.

A couple days later I went out for my daily exercise. Upon my return, lo and behold, my son said, Mom, Tyler Perry Studios called. I said stop playing with me boy. My son is a jokester and he knew about the prophetic word, I had received. Daddy God spoke to me about being in the Tyler Perry movie. I believed God. I told everyone even the JMI congregation about the Word from the Lord. My son handed me my phone and said, here mom listen. Sure enough, it was a message from Tyler Perry Studios (TPS) and they wanted to know if I was available for a film "The Family that Preys". Not too much detail, yet, you know I called right away. I spoke with this woman who congratulated me. She went on to say that I was selected to be in a wedding scene, after reviewing my photo. She asked me if I can come to Atlanta, GA, for a fitting. YESSSSSSSSSSSSSSS! Hello! She then said she would send me an email with the confirmation and more details. She was so kind and excited for me. Amen. Thank you Jesus. Hallelujah!

Speechless. Overjoyed. Overwhelmed. I thought to myself, Daddy said it and He's doing it. This is Father's word coming to past. I was still trying to figure out how they received my picture and my information. I had not gotten around to sending it. Truth came out afterward, my amazing daughter Micaela sent my information. Gotta love her.

I had shared the news with my friend (brother in Christ) Apostle T from Georgia about being in a Tyler Perry movie. He offered that I stay with him and his wife in their home. I did. It was only suppose to be a weekend timeframe for filming and the weekend turned into 2 weeks on set. Thank you Jesus and I will tell you why. "God is Just, but Favor isn't fair". A little humor there. Truly, Father's Will,

Divine Intervention, Supernatural Favor, Daddy God's promises that are Yes and Amen. Let me tell you why.

Arriving on set, I checked in, they fed us and they placed me in a holding room. It appeared as if there were over five hundred people from all over the world. I was waiting for them to check my wardrobe and my makeup. I sat in a quiet corner and I was reading a book. I was just so happy to be there and be considered so I beheld. Selah! So much activity, yet everyone knew there place, everyone knew their role. They worked in unity and were professional and organized. They respected each others functions and positions. All had their own responsibilities. They worked as a team and there was order.

Teamwork is something I know much about in the military after 23 years. There is teamwork in Kingdom of God and Heaven. There is teamwork in the Body of Christ. There is teamwork family. There is teamwork in ministry. I love it when people work together for a common goal, like manifesting the Kingdom of Heaven here on earth. Selah!

What I enjoyed the most about being there was that my Father God would be so mindful of me and grant me the desires of my heart. He would also have me there for His purpose, honor and glory at the same time.

Suddenly, this man came in front of me and asked me, Excuse me, Maam, What size are you? Now you know it is absolutely abnormal for a man to ask a woman what size are you? Strangers just don't do that, especially a man asking a woman. At first, I was taken back, but not only did he look important with his headpiece and radio in his pocket. He spoke as one having authority so I answered. I gave him the information and he responded with, great grab your stuff you're coming with me.

I didn't hesitate nor asked questions, I obeyed and followed him like the good soldier that I am. He than said, You are the new maid, the maid that we hired literally broke her leg. She's not coming and had to cancel. I said thank you Jesus and prayed and released healing to this woman. I didn't know her, yet prayed thanking Daddy God the entire time.

This man was the Assistant Director (AD) his name is George and now a current facebook friend of mine. He took me to a trailer with my own star on it. I cannot truly express in writing, except to shout, Hallelujah! Holy Spirit had to keep me together because of all the emotions, I was experiencing. It was better than winning the lottery. It was Daddy God's faithfulness manifesting right there and then, just for me.

Gratitude Break….Thank you Jesus. Tears of Joy. Sing unto the Lord a new song. Crazy Praise. Holy Spirit have your way always. Abba Father!

I immediately took pictures of my trailer and called my husband. I told him the great news. A weekend on set turned into 2 weeks. From wedding attendee, to Agnes (Kathy Bates' maid) in the movie. I was able to pray for people on set and speak prophetically into people's lives. It was an extraordinary mission. Tyler, if you are reading this, Daddy God is pleased with you. Keep up the great work. Keep it Holy. Keep it Real! Dream bigger! You know out of all people in the world, there is absolutely nothing impossible for "Our Daddy" God. I love you Tyler, and I pray for you always. Look forward to seeing the greater dimension you will pioneering in the years to come.

I was able to give Tyler a copy of my JMI Prayer list, while we were on set.

I wanted him to be encouraged and know that there are more for him than against him. Amen.

I became more involved in the Entertainment Industry to truly understand how it functions. I was intrigued with the Tyler Perry experience. I enjoyed the art and was able to help many others get work. I would like to state to all of you who enjoy going to the movies or television; it's not all glam. It's a lot of hard work for all involved. It requires commitment, perseverance and dedication to be successful. I honor you all and release favor to those in the Entertainment Industry, in Jesus name. Blessings and Peace be unto you.

This experience was nothing but God. Yes my Daddy God, always there, always here, still here today. My declaration is that these testimonies will inspire you to know that you can dream big. GOD IS BEYOND BIG! HE IS BIGGER THAN BIG! If you can do it yourself, you're not dreaming big enough. I love you Papa God. You are indescribable. GAGA GOOGOO! Infant state! Thank you Jesus, thank you Holy Spirit. I love you Lord!

CHAPTER **31**

Mission India – Luke 4:18

During Mission India, I've experienced many miracles. One incident stood out to me that transformed my life and manifested, truly unlocked another dimension in the Kingdom of Heaven. I went to preach on Luke 4:18. The Spirit of the LORD is upon me, because he hath anointed me to preach the gospel to the poor; he hath sent me to heal the brokenhearted, to preach deliverance to the captives, and recovering of sight to the blind, to set at liberty them that are bruised.

I went to the pulpit to preach, teach, share, and speak this Gospel. I opened up the Holy Bible (The Word of God) and I began to read. As I began to read something extraordinary happened. The Holy Spirit that's already within me, came upon me and consumed me. When I spoke those words, it was not I who spoke, I heard Jesus. I read it closed the book like Jesus did and sat down in the Messiah's chair. I could not control my feet, my mouth my hands. I felt like I was literally floating towards the chair and sat down. I would not consciously walk over and sit in the Messiah's chair but I did. Father, Jesus, Holy Spirit POSSESSED me like never before. Understand that when I spoke those words, it was like an echo. I was not even there. I was a vessel being used by my Daddy God, Jesus and Holy Spirit. His perfect will was done.

It was finished before it began. I stayed quiet and waited. I normally do this when I don't know what to do next. I will literally be quiet and sit in His presence and be still. Remember I am a soldier! No instructions, no movement. It has become supernaturally natural in me. Under reconstruction. Work in progress. LOL. It was Jesus' nature too. **John 5:19,30,31**. Jesus said, I do what I see My Father do. **John 12:49-50**, I do not speak from myself, but the Father who sent me, Himself who commands me what I should say and speak. LOL. Miracles signs and wonders began to break out in the meeting. I didn't have to lay hands on anyone. Heaven invaded earth. The glory cloud filled the placed. Healing and deliverance. It was easy. How amazing it is that the very presence of "Our Father, Jesus and Holy Spirit, in you to manifest in such a way that needs are met simultaneously. To witness and just be there in that awesome atmosphere was more than I could even ask or even think. You are an awesome wonder. I love you Lord.

CHAPTER **32**

Transfiguration

TRANSFIGURATION DEFINED: A complete change of form or appearance into a more beautiful or spiritual state. Christ appearance in radiant glory to three of his disciples. Metamorphis. An exalting, glorifying, or spiritual change. Holy Spirit have your way. **Matthew 17:2** There He (Jesus) was transfigured before them. His face shone like the sun and his clothes became as white as the light. You want me to share so I will. I was planning to share this in another book, yet, I will share now. Father knows why. If this has happened to you it is perfectly normal when the Kingdom of God manifests. I am sharing so that you can expect it to happen more so than not. I learned in my walk with Father, not to question certain things and just obey and release what He wants me to. I will be brief and let you (Selah)! For this revelation. You are Kings and Priests. **Proverbs 25:2** – It is the glory of God to conceal a thing; but the honor of Kings is to search out a matter.

There were two people who had witnessed my transfiguration. Christ showed up and they no longer saw me, they saw Christ in me, the hope of glory. I love this scripture. **Galatians 2:20** - I am crucified with Christ; and it is no longer I who liveth, but it is Christ who lives in me; And the life which I live now in the flesh, I live by faith in the Son of God, who loved me and gave himself for me. This transfiguration was not about me. Just like Jesus, He knew who He was. When you walk with Father God, you will transfigure before man and they too will believe. You have been advised. A voice from the cloud may or may not speak, Behold! Thy Kingdom come, Thy will be done on earth as it is in Heaven. Expect the supernatural to invade the natural, your natural world. Expect Heaven to invade earth. **Colossians 3:1-3 -** Since, then you have been raised with Christ, set your hearts on things above where Christ is seated at the right hand of God. Set your minds on things above, not on earthly things. For you died and your life is now HIDDEN with Christ in God. When Christ who is your life appears, then you will also appear with him in glory. Seek Father's will and obey Him quickly. Selah! Nuff said. I will wait upon the Lord.

Chapter 33

Jesus Is Still Here!

I have seen Jesus many times and in many different ways. Not one time is more spectacular than any other. All encounters are, eternally, life transforming.

I was at a conference in Rhode Island and it was during worship when behold Jesus appears. He was dressed from head to toe in Royal Apparel as the King of Kings and Lord of Lord. Majestic is His name. He was wearing a coat of arms of many colors. This coat of arms stretched out around Him so wide. It had pure white at the edge and hem all around. It was breath taking. I still see him like this now and then. You can never forget this glorious image of Jesus. Not ever. He had a large crown on His head, but not over exaggerated; I drew a picture of it and posted it on facebook. He was walking upright and slow with this grace that was unexplainable, yet perfect.

I wept in total awe and amazement. I gazed upon him unmovable, thinking within myself, if I move He may leave. I fixed my eyes on Jesus and did not want to look away. I continued to worship with my heart, not words. His appearance was mesmerizing. His walk was so confident yet, full of gratitude. Intriguingly abnormal. All I can muster to cry out and say was thank you Jesus. Thank you Jesus, thank you Jesus. I wanted to walk with Him and be with Him. Truth is He is walking with me and will always be. My Lord,

My Savior, My King. I want to see you more and more. I remember the very first time you came to my rescue. I reminisce of that day so much. The day I fell in love with you Jesus, because you loved me first. **1 John 4:19**. Thank you for the cross. Thank you for redeeming me back to "Our Father" to Yourself, by Your Spirit. You knew everything about me and didn't change Your Mind about me. You Jesus gave me Your Mind. I have all of You Jesus. I have the Mind of Christ.

1 Corinthians 2:16. I walk in divine health because You (Jesus) live in me. **Galatians 2:20**. You allowed me and empowered me to be a son of God. **John 1:12**. Thank you for your Mercy. Thank you for your Grace. Thank you for giving me a heart of flesh. **Ezekiel 36:26**. Thank you Jesus that I am full of your Compassion and Mercy, because you live in me. **Matthew 14:13-14**. Thank you Jesus that I am forgiven. **1 John 1:9**. Thank you for making me rich. **2 Corinthians 8:9**. Thank you for your Wisdom. Thank you for Truth. Thank you for Patience. Thank you for my family. Thank you for making me a partaker of Your death and resurrection. **Colossians 2:12**. I enter Your gates with thanksgiving and my lips with praise. **Psalm 100:4**. Thank you for the plans you have for me. **Jeremiah 29:11**. Thank you for being the perfect human example of faith, hope and love. I live to please you Father with the help of my savior Jesus, by Your Spirit. Thank you Jesus, You are still here. Holy Spirit continue to have your way. I AM Eternally grateful.

Several months ago, in Africa, I displayed my Tallit (Prayer Shawl) as I preached the Gospel of the Kingdom. I do this occasionally as directed by Holy Spirit or even just to provoke Daddy God to do good. Selah! I made a declaration that if anyone was to touch my Tallit, they would be healed. Example: Woman with the issue of blood, with Jesus. **Matthew 9:20** Apostle Paul's handkerchief. **Acts 19:11,12**. I further said whatever the need is in your life, come and touch the Tallit and receive your miracle.

Sure enough Jesus showed up and was seen by this man. He was a skeptic and shared how he saw Jesus standing where I was. He was honest to say He was a skeptic, yet, because He saw Jesus, he now believes. Awesome.

This other woman came to me after service and she said I touched your tallit and nothing happened. I asked her what was wrong. She said she has double vision. She sees two of everything. This illness has been like this for years and she said I am so tired of it. I asked you touched my tallit. She said OH YES, very adamantly. I said your faith has made you whole, now open your bible. She was standing by the gentlemen who saw Jesus. I said to her now read your bible with your new vision. She began to read, to her amazement and everyone else she read with exactly that "new vision". Double vision totally gone. Vision restored. All glory, honor and praise to you Father. Thank you Jesus for showing up. Thank you for what you've did on the cross, long ago, before the foundations of the earth. You thought of us and had us in mind. Oh merciful Jesus, how majestic you are. Jesus show up right now to the readers of this book. It is your book. It is all about you. Show up Jesus to them. Touch them in a way that they will never be the same. Touch them as they touch this book. Let them taste and see how really good you are. Let them behold you and transform them with your love. They want you they need you and they are reading this because you made it possible for them sweet Jesus. I LOVE YOU.

Manifest your glorious power in, through and around them. Embrace them with your Holy presence. Thank you for making them free. For who the Son (Jesus) sets and makes free is free indeed. You said in Mark 16:15-18, when your gospel in preached…. to those who believe, signs will follow. They believe. I believe for them. Whatever the need is I release it in the name of Jesus. Have your way Holy Spirit and manifest in Jesus name. Thank you Daddy God. You never leave me (us). You never forsake me (us). You are always here. You change not. Omnipresent Father God of Abraham, Isaac and Jacob. Thank you.

CHAPTER 34

Barren? Not!

In Saint Augustine Florida, I was ministering at Church on the Rock. During the altar call, the Pastors wife, said to me that she wanted to be a grandmother. She asked if I would pray for her daughter in law so that she can have babies. She brought her daughter in law to me and asked me to lay hands on her. She was doing all the talking so I wasn't sure if mother in law wanted babies or the daughter. What about you daughter, Do you want to have babies? Immediately, she cried, Yes and said she had tried and the doctors… Quickly, I said enough about the doctors. No disrespect, doctors, but my Daddy God, is the Final Authority with the Final Answer. Truth is, it was finished before it began (Selah!). In the Kingdom of Heaven there is no sickness infirmity or disease, especially barrenness. I asked again, are you sure you want babies? I am going to lay my hands on your belly and you will be fruitful and multiply. You will have babies and she replied Yes, just so emotionally. So I said congratulations and touched her belly. We both felt the fire of God with a touch. It was truly finished. I told her go home and make babies and loved on her with a hug.

A year later, there was an event, Christian Family picnic, at Treaty Park, and they were all present in attendance. I saw the young lady with her precious gift (her baby) in her arms and her husband (had the other baby) they had twins. Hallelujah! Isn't Our Daddy God totally and extraordinarily amazing. Only that He can! He cannot be anything but GOOD. He gives good gifts, always. Thank you Jesus.

CHAPTER 35

The Lame Walk!

Miracles, signs and wonders follow those who believe. In Africa, during this crusade, I walked up to a woman with her children. She was crippled for 4 years due to trauma in her physical body. I simply grabbed her hands and told her to get up in Jesus name and she did. She just got up so easily and began to walk with her children. They wept with joy. Glorious! It doesn't matter how many miracles and how many times supernatural things occur. Every time, every situation I am always awestruck when it happens. There are pictures of this incident, on our website. www.jesusmi.org. The joy of the Lord is truly my strength. Joy to me is far more than a feeling it is a personified and manifested in the way of Jesus. My Joy, My Peace, My everything, thank you Jesus for making all things great, new and possible. Thank you for your ever present help in our time of need. I honor you Jesus. Thank you Jesus for healing all. I AM eternally grateful.

CHAPTER 36

Tumor Dissolved Under My Hand

In Africa, during another Tallit (Prayer Shawl) event. Many miracles happened. Jesus is in the house. One in particular, I remembered, because to be quite honest, it kind of creeped me out. This man had a tumor on his chest below his heart. I asked him where is it so he grabbed my hand to show me and placed it on the tumor. This tumor disappeared and dissolved right underneath my hand. I felt it and it dissolved while my hand was on the tumor. Supernaturally! At the touch of the Master's (Jesus) hand, this man was instantly healed. There is a video on you tube of him sharing his testimony. See and hear for yourself. The Physician of all physicians lives in us. Jesus our Healer. He is still healing today, only believe. I believe for you. Tumors, Cancer, Aids (HIV) were defeated along time ago. Confess and agree with what Jesus did on the cross and receive your healing today. Amen. Jesus is the same yesterday, today and forever and changes not. He will manifest healing through you around you for you and for others. Only believe! Healing has already taken place and is available. Isaiah 53:5. Jesus is not going back on the cross. It is finished.

God is not a respecter of persons; He is a respecter of faith. Faith moves God. His Word says, according to your faith be it done unto you. **Matthew 9:29.** So they are definitely measures of faith, just as there is a diversity and uniqueness of His children. Don't ever compare yourself to anyone. Be the best representative and ambassador of the Kingdom of Heaven that you can be. Allow Jesus to always be your Mentor, Teacher, Role model, and Example, you will never go wrong. He does not only do this with me. He is faithful to His word. He is faithful to His promises. If you only believe. No other option. Only Believe! In order to come to Jesus, you must first believe that He Is! He is a rewarder of those who diligently seek Him. **Hebrews 11:6**. He is and was and is to come. He is here. He will always be here. He will never leave you or forsake (mislead) you. Christ in me, the hope of glory, writing this book. This book is written to inspire you to do the greater works, just like Jesus said you would as He works with you. **John 14:12**. This epistle (open book) is to encourage you to know that He is an ever present help in your time of need. He is faithful. He is real. He loves you with an everlasting love. Call on Him, I promise you He will answer. He is waiting for you to call on Him. Right now. Don't delay just obey and believe the good news (Gospel). Tomorrow is promised to no man. I tell you the truth because Jesus is the only way. He is love and I am love and love speaks truth. Love does not allow friends to go to hell. Love really cares about you. God is love. John 3:16. God loves you so much that He didn't spare His Son and it pleased Him to send His Son to the cross, just for you. You are worth the blood of Jesus. He made you worthy. Call on Him today. Jesus loves you and so do we.

CHAPTER 37

A Demon Called My Phone?!

I hate the devil and I am allowed to. I hate the deception that he brings; he is a liar and the father of it. Since this book is about Father God, Jesus and Holy Spirit, I must honor them and expose the devil. I will be brief and just hit the main points. A demon called me on my phone. My cell phone rang, I answered and a demon said, I am going to kill you and the person I am speaking through right now.

Not that this was humorous, yet, after, I laughed, I said, How dare he? The nerve of him. I told him to be quiet and come out. He continued to speak and I said again, Did you not hear me? Silence and shut your mouth. The young lady who dialed the phone finally cried out, HELP! I instructed her to fight and command the demons to be quiet so we can talk. She did and they obeyed. I made an appointment with her to meet and finish the process. The young lady was totally set free. I just attended her graduation, where she received her PHD in Divinity and Theology also graduated as Valedictorian of her class with a double major. She is a mighty woman of God. I look forward to see the great and incredible events that will be happening in her life. She has supernatural favor. Father God has kept us divinely connected for many years now. She was able to accompany JMI on our mission trips to Jerusalem, Bethlehem and Nazareth, this past year, also Guatemala. Her life is truly amazing. I am so grateful that I didn't hang up the phone.

She is a soul, like every soul out there to be won for the Kingdom of God. Please do not ever give up on people, for your own selfish comforts. If you don't understand them or believe you cannot help them, pass them on to someone who can. Jesus never gave up on us or anyone and He never will. Remember, in **John 17** as He spoke with "Our Daddy', Jesus said, I have kept all those you gave me, except the son of perdition, which was the plan from the beginning. If Jesus kept them all so should we.

CHAPTER 38

As You Go...

In Rhode Island we were on our way to a powerful conference manifesting miracles signs and wonders. In the lobby of the hotel, where we stayed I noticed this couple and they were signing (language). I went to her and said hello and smiled. She smiled back and I asked can you hear me? She responded a little, I am deaf in one ear. I began to tell her that God gave her 2 ears to hear, not 1 and if she would like to experience that, she said sure. Thank you Jesus.

I asked her to tell me which ear was blocked. This one and she motioned to the ear. I said, when I snap my fingers 3 times near this ear, on the 3rd snap, your ear will open. You will hear and than you can come with us to the conference. She smiled, yet was expectant. 1, 2, 3, after the third click, she yelled in OUCH, that was loud. LOL. She was able to hear with both ears now. I invited her to the conference and her and her entire family came and enjoyed the conference. She was so happy, yet, mentioned that sound was a bit loud. I just asked God to adjust and bring balance in Jesus name and He did. Jesus healed all when He walked the earth. The Healer is always at work ready to transform someone's life for their good and to glorify "Our Father" in heaven. Look and Look again and for opportunities to manifest Jesus. Thank you Jesus for your faithfulness and working with us. I love you.

This book, if you have not noticed by now is interactive. It does not matter what your issue is? If it has a name, IT HAS BEEN DESTROYED A LONG TIME AGO. IT HAS BEEN DEFEATED, DESTROYED, REMOVED, CANCELLED, ANILIATED, STRUCK DOWN in the mighty name of Jesus. The name above every name JESUS! JESUS! JESUS said "IT IS FINISHED and it truly is. Declare and decree this truth over your issue and receive your miracle, healing, deliverance today. There is nothing, no one greater than the name of Jesus. No one can do you like Jesus. Jesus is more than enough and all you need. He is the only One that will restore, realign, reconstruct your life to its original state of dominion and ownership, only believe!

CHAPTER 39

Intercessory Prayer (Divine Intervention)

My friend and I went to fellowship at the local church building in New Jersey (NJ). He had many questions about my love for Jesus so I invited him and he came. When we arrived, we enjoyed Praise and Worship. He was in the military with me, stationed at McGuire AFB, NJ. He was drawing nigh to the Lord and the Lord was drawing nigh to him. After praise and worship, he wanted to leave. I said, Oh no, this is the best part of the service. This is where you learn. He still insisted on leaving. He wanted me to leave forcefully and shrugged me to leave. I kindly said, I am staying and I will see you at work tomorrow. His countenance did not look well and he left frustrated and bothered.

This was not good. Immediately, Father told me to pray. I began to pray by Holy Spirit. On my knees, I prayed uncontrollably in Tongues. I had never prayed in this way before. Two things I knew for sure:

1. I was interceding on behalf of the soldier
2. The gentlemen would be OK.

The next day, I was at work and my friend came to me and asked, What did you do to me? He seemed bewildered, happy, yet a bit afraid. I replied, Excuse me? He proceeded to say, when I left the church, on my way home, I had a head to head collision with my truck and the truck was totally destroyed. I didn't get not one scratch and the other driver either. The truck is totally destroyed, yet not one glass shattered. I smiled and responded, I didn't do anything, Papa God, spared your life. Thank Him! Thank Jesus! All I did was obeyed and prayed. I explained to him that after you left the church Papa God, told me to pray and I prayed like I never prayed before. It was my first time. I said I am sorry about your truck, but I am grateful to God, that you are alive and well. He smiled and said thank you. He knew Jesus saved his life, again. Thank you Jesus. I love you.

CHAPTER **40**

Driving On Empty

I have been licensed as a Real Estate Broker for almost 20 years. I remember when I studied to take the exam. The desire was birthed out of a crooked real estate transaction, when I purchased my own home. The real estate person not honest. Mercy! I talked to Papa God about it because I talk to Him about everything. Great habit to get into. Actually He talks to me all the time. I cannot turn Him off, He's eternal. I need to hear Him. He told me if, you don't like it change it. Then Jesus chimed in and said, I have given you all power and authority to change everything that does not line up with My Kingdom. Become an honest Real Estate Broker. My response OK. Thank you Jesus.

In my life, when I don't know what to do, I pray, yet when I have clarity from Daddy God, I do it all in the name of Jesus, empowered by Holy Spirit.

So I inquired, study and prepared for my real estate exam. The day of my exam, I missed a passing score by a few questions. They printed the results, it reflected Failed. I was not happy, I was truly sad, sometimes in life, when we hear the Lord and obey; we expect things to be so easy, especially, when it was Papa God's idea. He told me to do it. Selah!

I studied again and immediately went back and took it again, this time I missed the passing grade by 1. The examiner gave me my results and it reflected Failed.

I walked away sorrowful and began to pout, sulk, and even question, myself, and asked, Did I really hear God? Was it His voice or mine? What am I doing? I was communicating within myself, with myself (ever been there) LOL. I got in my car to drive home. Still pouting, still sulking and not happy, blaming the examiner, a computer error, even my own memory, because I truly believed I studied hard and God is never to blame.

Here comes Papa in His "Still small voice"

DIALOGUE: God: Worship Me!

Me: I said nope, I am not happy right now, like a little child.

God: Worship Me, put on your Worship CD and Worship Me. I said again, No I am so angry right now, Daddy God. (Tears rolling down my face). You said to get my license. You said to change things and become an honorable Real Estate Broker. I heard you clearly Daddy and I am truly sad right now. I cannot worship even if I tried. (Still weeping).

I continued and began talking to Jesus because Daddy God silenced Himself. I don't understand Jesus you're always here for me. What happened? You always help me. I went on like a crazy person, yet, still in His presence. Jesus said, look at your gas tank. I immediately looked and I was on E (Empty) and had to drive about 50 miles to get home. I was on E with the gas light on. Mercy, Mercy Mercy! I came to myself. LOL

I quickly put my CD on and began to **WORSHIP** Abba Father for real and received His Mercy. Yes, He smiled at me. He is a Great Father. He understood that I had lost (the mind of Christ) and lived in my mind for a brief moment. He understood and He was not surprised. He is all knowing. Our Father God, is so amazingly Patient and Good and Merciful and Loving and Longsuffering and

Kind, and Incredible and Forgiving and Patient. Wait a minute did I say Patient and Merciful and Good and Loving and Kind and... Lol. Truly, He got me home on E (EMPTY) celestial gas (lol) and restored me the entire time. I WORSHIPPED Him and we laughed all the way home. Driving on empty, yet full of Him. His Grace! Thank you Jesus. Thank you Holy Spirit. Thank you Daddy God, You are amazing and I am so in love with You!

The next day, I decided to give myself a break from studying and go shopping. I went to this antique thrift store that I driven by several times, yet I never stopped in to see. I went in only to find myself involved in another divine encounter. I like going to these type stores because, in life, one man's junk may be another man's treasure. You never know what you may find and I like surprises. I went into the store only to experience another angel encounter.

The owner of the store was truly an angel incognito. When I walked in the store, I felt the power and the presence of God so strong, that I was walking slow. I wanted to experience every detail of what was taking place. This woman was radiant in appearance and was by herself. She stared at me as I came nearer to her. I said, Hello. She said, how can I help you, are you looking for something in particular? I said, no, just browsing. She said, don't be sad and don't cry anymore, you will get your license. At this point, every hair on my body was at attention. I had chills. I said excuse me. Now, I heard her, yet I needed to hear her again. What are you saying to me, Maam? Do I know you? She responded, no, but I know you. What do you think God is just going to give you a license? You have to know like you know baby girl? It's the only way to protect and help His children. You have to know real estate.

Total stranger, meeting me for the first time, speaking prophetically into my life. I was there but I was not there, I was overwhelmed. Stunned. Speechless and deeply moved and touch by Daddy God, once again. How mindful He is of me that He would orchestrate this encounter in such a unconceivable way. How can you not love "Our Father" like this. He is so worthy of our love. She went on to say. Jesus will help you but you have to do your part. She went on to share a testimony with me and said:

TESTIMONY: One day I was here by myself in the store and no one was around. I was having a heart attack and I cried out for help. Jesus came down from heaven and put His hand into my heart and He pulled out the heart attack out of my body with His hand. He helped me but it was my faith, my cry out to Him, and I had to open my mouth, for His hand. No one was around to help me and He intervened on my behalf. I literally saw and felt it come out of my mouth. God says cry out to me and I will hear you. I will answer you. I heard Him and obeyed. I did my part and He did His.

I listened in awe and was still trying to grasp, in all creation what was happening here. I didn't want to miss a thing. She ended with now go and study and do your part. She gave me instructions and said, Ask Him, what am I missing, Lord? What do I really need to know? Trust Him and you will pass.

So grateful. I loved on her and held her and didn't want to let her go. Totally amazed and in awe of the great I AM, Jesus and Holy Spirit. We were so blessed.

I got home and went before the Lord and asked, "What do I need to know?" He was clear. It was not the What? But the Why? Why do you want to get your real estate license, because I said so, or because you truly want to help my children? Purpose! I responded as He knew I would. I went to take the test and it was not only too easy, I did the test in record time. Confidently, I went to the woman and told her I know I passed as she graded me. I was smiling because I was leaving that place as a Licensed Real Estate Sales Associate and I did. Thank you Jesus. I placed my license with a reputable real estate company and in 1 year, I had my Real Estate Brokers License. I opened up Good Faith Realty, Inc., still active and in operation today. Consultant based and mostly charitable helping those in need. I help those who cannot afford real estate fees. Daddy God is amazing and is always patient, loving and kind. Jesus an ever present help in our time of need. Thank you Holy Spirit.

Chapter 41

You Will Live And Not Die!

My son and I and another sister in Christ decided to go for a jog. When we returned, we went into the living room and my son went into the bathroom. From the living room, we heard a big bang and a loud noise in the bathroom. The door was unlocked so the young lady ran to the bathroom and yelled Ma; you need to call the ambulance. I looked at her face full of panic and went to the bathroom. I found my son on the floor, in a seizure; blood and his eyes were in the back of his head, no pupils, all white. Mercy!

My son is bigger, taller and weighed a lot more than me. I cried out Jesus, as I bent over to grab my son by his T-Shirt and picked him up like a piece of paper. Supernatural Strength! Hallelujah! I placed him against the wall and said Samuel, look at me. You will live and not die! His pupils quickly came back. He looked at me and the seizure and blood stopped immediately. He came to himself and rubbed his head. I asked him what happened? He said, I felt dizzy and fell down and must have hit my head with the sink. No big deal, mom. He laughed as if it was funny. Like nothing happened. I said let me check your head and didn't I tell you to hydrate. Lol. He did have a small cut and wanted to go to the hospital for stitches, even though the bleeding had stopped. The young lady was beside herself and asked how did you pick him up, Ma? Jesus! Was and is and will always be my answer. He is the Answer! She kept repeating Father God! Thank you Jesus for divine intervention. The

Physician, the master Healer was in the house and did the work. Thank you for allowing me to be the vessel, You chose to restore my son. My gift from You (Daddy God) I love you eternally. My son has experienced so many miracles in his life. I know one day he will be able to share them all with the world. I love you Samuel, son of God. You are amazing! Thy Kingdom come Thy will be done in Samuel's life eternally, in Jesus name.

CHAPTER **42**

Your Worth Is In The Blood Of Jesus!

All are valuable. All are worth the blood of Jesus. The same blood Jesus shed for me, He shed for you. You are relevant. You may not know it, yet it does not negate or change the truth that Jesus died for you. You matter to the Kingdom of God, on earth right now as it is in Heaven. Take your rightful place of inheritance in the Kingdom of Heaven. You are a joint heir with Christ Jesus. Take your place! If you are reading this right now, it is not too late. Repent for the Kingdom of Heaven is at hand.

Jesus valued all. He valued (You and I). While we were yet sinners, He died for us, not when we had it all together. While we were in our sinful lifestyle, ignorantly, not knowing our identity, He went to the cross. He counted it all joy too. Love never gives up and love never fails, nor quits. It is "Our Father's will to love Him with all that He is and love our neighbor as ourselves. LOVE is the **<u>KEY</u>** to unlocking our priestly and royal inheritance in the Kingdom, on earth as it is in Heaven. Love is the key for eternal happiness with Father God, Jesus and Holy Spirit. I have the keys, Daddy God gave it to me and it's available for you too. Jesus gave it to Peter the keys to the Kingdom of Heaven **Matthew 16:19** and the Giver of keys lives in me (Selah!) Does He live in you? If not, He can. Just open (unlock) the door of your heart and let Him in.

Revelation 3:20 – Here I am! I stand at the door and knock. If anyone hear my voice and opens the door, I will come in and eat with that person and they with me. (He is Still Here) Present and accounted for. Reliable! Dependable! Open up and let Him in. Patiently longing for you to know Him and get into a relationship with Him.

Like I shared with you before, God is no respecter of persons. I believe that as you read this book, you were able to relate to some of the testimonies and experiences with me. I am sure you have many of your own. I am here to tell you that you need to tell the world. I am doing that right now. You need to tell the world, God is here. He was there in the beginning and He will be here in the end. He is the Alpha and Omega. He is here, right now. He is with you right where you are. He is everywhere at the same time. He is with you and He is with me. He is waiting for you to say yes to Him and no to the devil, once and for all. No man can serve two masters: **Matthew 6:24** for either he will hate the one and love the other; or else he will hold to the one and despise the other. He loves you and created you for His purpose and for His glory. His plans are to prosper you in every area of your life. Thy Kingdom come Thy will be done to the reader Father God. I thank you for their life. I know that after reading this book they will never be the same. You made it possible and I am grateful. I appreciate you Lord. Holy Spirit have your way in Jesus name.

CHAPTER 43

Mercy Said No!

Create in them a clean heart and a right spirit within them. Fill them with your compassion for souls, Father God. I am still here. God knows the many times that the enemy tried over and over again to take my life. God said no, mercy said no. God said, I have much need of you. I asked God, Why me? He answered, because you surrendered your will and sought Mine. Like a child, you believed My Word. You came to Me believing, Who I AM. You embraced My Son when He knocked, you opened the door. You loved me back by your obedience even when you thought you were going the right way, you did everything unto Me. Your heart is pure before Me. You have no hidden agendas. You love My people. You thirst and hunger after Righteousness. You trust Me. You purpose to please Me and I trust you with My riches. You draw nigh to Me daily. You are grateful. I AM your Confidence. I can go on with the Why? Yet is this enough and I said Yes Daddy, with tears in my eyes and joy in my heart. He then said, I will manifest myself in ways that they won't be able to deny Me. I will overwhelm you. I love you baby girl, now rest in My Bosom.

CHAPTER **44**

Who Do You Pray To?

Praise be to Father God, Jesus, Holy Spirit. I don't know if you notice, how I include all three and don't neglect to make mention of one or the other. There is a reason why they are 3 in 1, yet their functions are uniquely different. Jesus did not consider it robbery to be equal with God and neither do I? **Philippians 2:5-6**. Why should I? Jesus is my perfect example and I am to emulate Him. God did not die on the cross, Jesus did. **John 19:30**. Jesus did not create the heavens and the earth, God did. **Genesis 1:1**. God created mankind. **Genesis 1:27**. Jesus was there, yet, God created us in His image and the likeness of His Son (Jesus). Selah! He is truly my Daddy God and defines all that I am and trusted me with His (DNA) Divine Never-ending Anointing. His Divine Sperm is permanently in me. **1 John 3:9**. AMPC. God poured out His Spirit upon all flesh (in me and upon me) for His good pleasure, for His will, for His purpose, For all mankind. **Joel 2:28**

I asked someone very dear to me one day. Who do you pray to? She responded Jesus, now we know biblically speaking; Jesus never prayed to himself. We know that God the Father, Jesus the Son and His Holy Spirit are all ONE (Trinity). Jesus (as our example) walked the earth. Jesus is the Way to the Father. When He walked the earth (JESUS WAS ALL HUMAN). He lived a life of prayer and fasting, yet He prayed to "Our Father". He represented Father God in all perfection. Jesus is the ONLY WAY to the Father. So I choose to follow His perfect example to pray to "Our Father in Jesus name and allow Holy Spirit to intervene whenever Holy Spirit needs has to. The Holy Spirit leads us and guides us into all truth. **John 16:13**. Amen. When asked, Lord, teach us how to pray. Jesus told them, When you pray say Father, hallowed be Your name. **Luke 11:1- 2**. Our example, Jesus addressed "Our Father" in His teaching. Father God gave Jesus, His Son the name above every name. Whatsoever we ask the Father, in (His) Jesus name, He will do it. **John 14:13-14**. It is important how you pray, be so mindful, so your prayers are answered. Thank you Holy Spirit.

CHAPTER **45**

Streets Of Gold On Earth

Prophetic dreams, visions, words are inevitable when you are in a relationship with Papa God. He is always talking. His nature is CREATIVE and He cannot help but show you His artistic talent. Lol. Truly He is His Word and His Word is Eternal. He cannot and will not stop so listen! Words create pictures and so forth. Ok, Nuff said. I shared that to say that although there have been many prophetic dreams, visions and words, God wanted me to share this one with you.

I was at the JMI mission home in Palatka, Florida and I had a dream. In this vision, I saw my land (about 2 acres) and I was thinking within myself all the work that had to be done to clear it. I kept hearing the Lord say, that my land was holy land and the grounds were holy grounds. I heard this before the dream and during the dream. He then showed me streets of pure gold so thick, yet incredibly pure. It looked like an ice-skating rink; except it was pure solid gold and people were walking on it. People of all walks of life. I saw tennis shoes, heels, sandals, and even no shoes at all.

It was not a crowd; it was a few feet walking on it at one time. I asked the Lord, where is this place Daddy? Are you putting it on my land? I would just love it here. Your children can come and enjoy like a prayer park. He said to me, My Kingdom come, My will be done. I responded with on earth as it is in Heaven. Yes, He said, there will be streets of gold that will be walked on, on earth as it is in Heaven. He then said get ready.

I came out of this dream and shared it with my husband. I then traveled to Jacksonville, Florida to go to a Christian bookstore. I met a young lady who said that the Prophets in Jacksonville, Florida called for investment of gold before October 2017. Your guess is as good as mine? I am sure Papa God is about to do something great and big for His children. Look and look again.

Dreams and visions. **1 Corinthians 14:24, 25 and Joel 2:28**. I've had many prophetic dreams and visions, which is normal in a relationship with Father God, Jesus Holy Spirit. Too many to mention here, yet this one dream I had where God took me into His Bosom (a place of safety) and showed me Hell. This dream is worth sharing because it came with a warning. God said, tell My People. He didn't just say the world or certain religious groups or ethnic cultures. He said tell My people, that there is a way that seems right to a man… I knew the rest of the verse. **Proverbs 14:12**. But its end is the way of death. Beloved, Hell is a real place. I saw fire in the form of mankind, lava and darkness. I heard the weeping and gnashing of teeth. **Matthew 13:42.** Many will say to me on that day, Lord, Lord did we not prophesy in your name and in your name drive out demons and in your name perform many miracles? Then I will say plainly to them, I NEVER KNEW YOU… **Matthew 7:23**. Saints listen to me please; DO NOT USE THESE MANIFESTATIONS ALONE, AS A SIGN THAT YOU HAVE ARRIVED AND YOUR SALVATION IS SECURE. Talk to Jesus. It is as simple as asking Jesus for help. Ask Holy Spirit to help you **KNOW** Jesus for real. In Spirit and in Truth. Ask Jesus to take your heart and receive His in exchange. Tell Jesus how you want to **KNOW** Him intimately, in every way. Study His life (The Gospels) **Matthew Mark, Luke and John**. He is your friend. He will show up. Jesus will help you. He is the Author and the Finisher of your Faith. Jesus loves you more than you can ever imagine. Trust Jesus and know that "Our Father" God has already made this possible. It's easy, but not in your own strength. Be confident and remember, if you ask Him anything according to His will, which it is His will to

KNOW Him and walk with Him. HE HEARS YOU AND YOU HAVE IT. **1 John 5:14-15**. Thank you Jesus!

Daddy God is real. He is the same yesterday today and forever, He is and was and is to come. He changes not and He is always here, Omnipresent, Omniscience and Omnipotent. Whatever He is up to it is for our good and His glory. I look forward with faith, hope and in love, believing for there is no other option in Christ Jesus. Seeking the Kingdom first, **Matthew 6:33**. Thank you so much for saving me from me and having Your Way (Jesus) in my life. Thank you Holy Spirit (My Comforter) discerner of all spiritual things. I am dependent on you Holy Spirit and surrender all than I am to Your Divine and Perfect Will Daddy God in Jesus name. I AM Eternally grateful.

CHAPTER **46**

I Am Still Here!

I AM STILL HERE – WHY? BECAUSE ALTHOUGH – IT IS FINISHED – DADDY GOD IS NOT FINISHED WITH ME YET! I LOOK FORWARD TO EVERY WAKING SECOND, MINUTE, HOUR, DAY, WEEK, MONTH, YEAR IN TOTAL SURRENDER AND SUBMISSION TO YOUR WILL FOR YOUR PEOPLE, IN LOVE AND IN YOUR BOSOM, DOING YOUR WILL, WITHOUT COMPROMISE, IN SPIRIT AND IN TRUTH, I WORSHIP YOU DADDY GOD AND IT IS IN YOU THAT I LIVE AND MOVE AND HAVE MY BEING JESUS. I EXIST BECAUSE AND FOR YOU! IT IS A PRIVILEGE AND AN HONOR TO SERVE YOU IN ALL THINGS. YOU COMPLETE ME DADDY GOD, THANK YOU FOR YOUR SON (JESUS) MY SAVIOUR FOREVER, MY FRIEND, MY HEART, MY WAYMAKER, MY PROMISE KEEPER, MY LION AND LAMB, MY KING. THANK YOU FOR SHOWNG UP IN MY LIFE WHEN I NEEDED YOU THE MOST AND YOU HAVE NEVER LEFT ME, CONDEMNED ME, NOR FORSOOK ME. YOU ARE MY TRUTH, MY LIGHT, MY ROCK, MY MODEL, MENTOR, TEACHER, HERO, HEALER AND DELIVERER. YOU ARE MY EXAMPLE FOR LIFE. I LOVE YOU JESUS AND I LOOK FORWARD TO MANY AND SPLENDID MORE MIRACLES TOGETHER.

THANK YOU FOR ALL THAT YOU DID FOR ME TO RESTORE ME AND RECONCILE ME BACK TO DADDY GOD. I KNOW I WOULD NOT BE HERE WITHOUT YOU AND I WILL SHOW YOU MY GRATITUDE FOREVERMORE.

THANK YOU HOLY SPIRIT. LIKE JESUS, I CANNOT DO ANYTHING APART FROM YOU. HE NEEDED YOU AND WAS BORN OF YOU RAISED BY YOU FROM THE GRAVE AND YOU WERE WITH HIM AT THE CROSS. YOU MADE IT POSSIBLE FOR JESUS AND YOU MAKE ALL THINGS POSSIBLE FOR ME. ALWAYS SHOWING UP AND INTERCEDING ON BEHALF OF FATHER'S CHILDREN, SONS, KING AND PRIESTS. I SUBMIT TO YOUR LEADING AND GUIDANCE. I SUBMIT TO YOUR REVELATION AND KNOWLEDGE OF MY FATHER, DAILY, BY YOUR SPIRIT. HAVE YOUR WAY ALWAYS IN JESUS NAME. I LOVE YOU AND NEED YOU HOLY SPIRIT!

I know without a doubt your life has been totally transformed. You have been touched by (Truth) Jesus. You are healed, delivered, and made free for your good and God's glory. You too will become and vessel of honor to be used by Daddy God in a supernatural way. You will. It is done. It is finished, I said it and you cannot change it, in Jesus name. I love you forever and Jesus LOVES YOU MORE! Please call us at 904.377.9351 and/or visit us on the website at www. jesusmi.org. Share your testimony of how the testimonies in this book has changed your life, send us an email to jesusministries1@ gmail.com

If you know anyone who cannot purchase this book. We will sow into their lives, please let us know. We look forward to hearing the great and wonderful testimonies. The miracles signs and wonders that Father God allowed to birth out of this epistle. I am so grateful that you invested in your life, there is so much more to share, because "Our Father" is so much more. Thank you again for reading His glorious book. Jesus made it possible and I truly enjoyed sharing!

Stay encouraged and inspired and know that although there are many miracles signs and wonders (like Jesus) many have not been included in this book. I can go on and on, just like His Word, which is eternal. As long as I have breathe, I will continue to write about "My Father's goodness, everlasting love and generous nature. I believe in you, because He believes in you. Please understand that all you have to do is dare to believe Him, His Word, His Son, like a little child and know and truly believe that there is nothing impossible for God. Fear not, only believe and watch what Daddy God will do in Jesus name, by Holy Spirit. I AM STILL HERE!

Mark 16:15-18 [15]He said to them, "Go into all the world and preach the gospel to all creation. [16]Whoever believes and is baptized will be saved, but whoever does not believe will be condemned. [17]And these signs will accompany those who believe: In my name they will drive out demons; they will speak in new tongues; [18]they will pick up snakes with their hands; and when they drink deadly poison, it will not hurt them at all; they will place their hands on sick people, and they will get well."

I leave you with this question, Who is greater the altar or the one who created the altar? Selah!

Peace be unto you!